CORPORATE DRAFTING
A PRACTICAL APPROACH

■ ■ ■

by

Stacey Bowers, JD, PhD
University of Denver
Sturm College of Law

AMERICAN CASEBOOK SERIES®

Mat #41528271

American Casebook Series is a trademark registered in the U.S. Patent and Trademark Office.

© 2015 LEG, Inc. d/b/a West Academic
    444 Cedar Street, Suite 700
    St. Paul, MN 55101
    1-877-888-1330

West, West Academic Publishing, and West Academic are trademarks of West Publishing Corporation, used under license.

Printed in the United States of America

ISBN: 978-0-314-29013-7

To Jeff

ACKNOWLEDGMENTS

I am grateful to everyone who assisted me with this book. In particular, I want to thank Zoie Springer for her support and encouragement of my endeavor to undertake this project. She provided invaluable assistance as my research assistant and continued those efforts significantly even after her graduation. I also want to thank my current research assistant Wil Henderson for his commitment to this project. Both Zoie and Wil provided excellent input, comments, and revisions and ultimately made this a better book. I also want to thank all of my corporate drafting students through the years who offered insight into how to make many of these drafting exercises better. Additionally, thanks to the University of Denver Sturm College of Law and my colleagues for their support and encouragement of this project.

INTRODUCTION

A critical skill for any aspiring transactional lawyer is the ability to draft contracts pertaining to different types of deals. One way for students to develop and perfect their drafting skills is to engage in a variety of different drafting exercises.

The goal of this book is to create drafting opportunities for students in a simulated practice world context. This book utilizes a merger and acquisition scenario as the underlying deal and asks students to draft various provisions of, and documents relating to, a merger and acquisition transaction. The drafting exercises in this book range from short assignments requiring students to draft a particular provision of the merger and acquisition agreement, such as the merger consideration provision, or an ancillary document such as an officer's certificate, to longer assignments requiring students to draft a letter of intent or employment agreement.

This book was developed and structured so that a professor desiring to teach a corporate drafting course from the perspective of a merger and acquisition had all of the necessary tools. The book leads off with a chapter that provides a brief overview of the main components of a merger and acquisition agreement. The second chapter of the book sets forth the basic fact scenario for the underlying transaction, including a detailed description of each company, its corporate structure and governance, an overview of its business, and limited financial information. Each subsequent chapter is designed as a stand-alone drafting exercise based upon the underlying fact scenario. The book includes 29 potential drafting assignments and allows the professor to select the assignments he or she chooses to utilize during the course of the semester. Though the chapters and assignments build upon one another, they do not require the professor to utilize them all or in a particular order for the book to function effectively. In some instances however, additional instruction may be required by the professor in lieu of an earlier chapter's exercise that was not undertaken. The professor may also utilize the underlying fact scenario to create additional drafting assignments not included in the book.

The drafting exercise chapters all follow the same format:

1. Each chapter leads off with a short description of the provision, contract, or form that is to be drafted in order to provide the student with background information and context.

2. Part 1 sets out the drafting assignment and indicates which company's outside counsel the student is working for in regard to that particular assignment.

3. Part 2 provides any additional facts needed to undertake the drafting assignment.

4. Part 3 contains a list of resources the student might consult to supplement their knowledge about and to help them prepare the particular drafting assignment.

TABLE OF CONTENTS

———

CORPORATE DRAFTING
A PRACTICAL APPROACH

CHAPTER 1

BASIC COMPONENTS OF A MERGER AND ACQUISITION AGREEMENT

■ ■ ■

There are many ways in which a merger and acquisition transaction can occur. As a result, mergers and acquisitions come in all shapes and sizes. The most common structures for these transactions are generally either as a straight stock purchase or some form of a merger. Within each of these structures there are a variety of ways to complete the transaction.

While each merger and acquisition transaction is unique, every transaction requires an extensively negotiated agreement. This chapter provides an overview of the main components of a merger and acquisition agreement, including the role of each provision.

Agreement Title

Most agreements contain some type of title at the top of the first page or on a stand-alone cover sheet that indicates the type of contract the document reflects. In order for a title to have value and meaning, it cannot simply be something generic such as "Agreement." While it is true that the document is an agreement that moniker does not provide the reader with any insight as to the content of the contract. The title should clearly indicate what this particular agreement addresses. In regard to a merger and acquisition, the title of the agreement might be any of the following: Merger and Acquisition Agreement; Merger Agreement; Acquisition Agreement; Merger Agreement and Plan of Merger; Stock Purchase Agreement; or another adequately descriptive title.

Introductory Paragraph

An introductory paragraph appears in most merger and acquisition agreements. This initial paragraph generally restates the type of agreement being entered into, identifies all the parties to the transaction, indicates each party's state of incorporation, and stipulates the date of the contract. The contract date may be the date of execution or another specified effective date and should include language that specifically makes the date reference clear. In many cases, the introductory paragraph also sets forth the defined terms to be used within the agreement to identify the parties.

1

Recitals and Lead-In

After the introductory paragraph, it is common to include a list of recitals that generally begin with the term "whereas." These recitals set forth the background information and provide context for the transaction. The recitals often help to clarify the parties' intentions for entering into the agreement and can provide guidance as to the contract's underlying purpose.

Some common recitals in a merger and acquisition agreement include the following: (i) statements regarding the nature of the transaction and why the parties are entering into the transaction; (ii) a stipulation that the board of directors of each company believes that the transaction is fair and in the best interest of the shareholders; (iii) a stipulation that the respective boards of directors have voted in favor of the transaction; (iv) a statement that the transaction meets certain tax requirements; and (v) a statement that the parties desire to make certain representations, warranties, and covenants in connection with the transaction.

Immediately after the recitals, there is a lead-in sentence that indicates that the parties agree to the terms that are set forth next, meaning the entire body of the agreement.

The Merger

One of the most important components of the merger and acquisition agreement is the merger section. This section sets forth exactly how the merger will be effectuated between the parties. It also indicates the underlying structure of the merger; meaning that it indicates if the structure is a straight merger, a triangular merger, a reverse triangular merger, or some other type of structure.

The merger section also sets forth the date and location of closing, that the certificate of merger will be filed with the applicable secretary of state offices, and the effective time of the closing. It also indicates the "effect of the merger" meaning that all the debts, liabilities, and duties of the company being purchased become the obligations of the surviving entity.

Additionally, this section generally addresses what will happen to the certificate of incorporation and bylaws of the surviving entity upon consummation of the merger (in particular, it indicates that the certificate of incorporation and bylaws will be amended and designates the name of the surviving entity). It also designates the persons who will be the initial officers and directors of the surviving entity.

Effect of the Merger on the Capital Stock

There is typically a section in the agreement that specifically sets forth what occurs with all the entities' classes of stock as a result of the merger and acquisition. This section may stand alone or be included in the merger section discussed above. This provision stipulates how the stock of each entity involved in the transaction will be managed. Specifically, it addresses how shares of the company being purchased and merged will be exchanged for shares of the new subsidiary or acquiring entity. There is generally a formula for the conversion of the shares of stock and the maximum amount of shares that can be issued is stipulated. Additionally, this provision discusses how fractional shares are to be handled and how the old shares will be surrendered.

When relevant, this provision may also address how dissenting shares will be handled, meaning the shares of those stockholders who did not approve the merger and are not willing to exchange their shares as a part of the transaction as they have exercised their dissenter's rights. This may result in an appraisal rights section to indicate how such shares will be valued outside the transaction.

If applicable, this section will also address how stock options and warrants of the company being purchased or merged will be handled. In some circumstances, the options and warrants may simply be cancelled upon the effective date of the transaction. In other cases, the options and warrants may be converted into or exchanged for options and warrants of the new subsidiary or acquiring entity.

Merger Consideration

In some transactions, in addition to or in lieu of the conversion and issuance of new shares, the purchasing entity may also tender cash to the shareholders of the acquired entity. In that instance, there is typically a provision that deals with the additional merger consideration, though in some cases it may be included in one of the two previous sections. The merger consideration provision sets forth the amount of cash consideration and how it will be disbursed. The cash consideration could simply be cash paid at closing or it could be tied to some type of calculation such as an earn-out payment based upon how the surviving entity continues to operate post-merger.

Representations and Warranties of Seller

Most merger and acquisition agreements, including a straight stock purchase or a merger, contain a representations and warranties section for the seller. This is true whether the whole company is being sold as a part of a stock purchase or as a merger. In some transactions, particularly if the seller is a closely held entity, the selling shareholders may also be required to make certain representations and warranties.

Typical seller representations and warranties found in a merger and acquisition agreement include many of the following: (i) organization and corporate existence; (ii) authority; (iii) consents and approvals of third parties; (iv) financial statements and SEC reports, if relevant; (v) no default; (vi) no undisclosed liabilities; (vii) litigation; (viii) compliance with applicable law; (ix) employment and labor matters; (x) environmental laws and regulations; (xi) tax matters; (xii) title to property; (xiii) intellectual property; (xiv) material agreements; and others.

Representations and Warranties of Buyer (could be both the parent entity and merger subsidiary)

Both the parent entity and newly formed subsidiary, if applicable, also make certain representations and warranties though these often seem minimal when compared to those made by the selling company. Typical buyer representations and warranties found in a merger and acquisition agreement include the following: (i) organization and corporate existence; (ii) capitalization; (iii) authority; (iv) required filings and consents; (v) compliance with applicable laws; (vi) no conflicts; (vii) financial statements and SEC reports, if relevant; (viii) availability and ownership of shares; and others.

Covenants

Most merger and acquisition agreements contain a covenants section. This section stipulates what the seller can and cannot do with the business from the time the merger and acquisition agreement is entered into until such time as the transaction is completed and the closing takes place.

These covenants are meant to protect the buyer from the seller injuring or depleting the assets of the business. Typical covenants include the following: (i) seller will continue to conduct its business as it has done in the past and will not make any material changes to the manner in which it conducts the business; (ii) seller agrees to allow buyer access to books, records, and other information regarding the seller's business or its assets; (iii) seller agrees to notify buyer of any material changes; (iv) seller agrees to take whatever continuing actions need to be taken to ensure that the transaction takes place, such as obtaining regulatory approvals or third party consents; (v) seller agrees to keep the terms of the transaction confidential and to work with the buyer to make proper public disclosure, often through a press release; (vi) seller agrees to make any tax or financial disclosure filings that are required; (vii) seller or its high level employees often agree not to compete with buyer after the closing of the merger and acquisition; and other pertinent covenants that the parties agree to include.

Closing Conditions

Included in all types of merger and acquisition agreements is a section that addresses the various parties' obligations in regard to closing. The seller, as well as the buyer and buyer subsidiary, if applicable, must meet certain conditions before the other side is obligated to close the deal.

Generally the seller requires the following conditions to be met prior to or as of the closing date: (i) that all the representations and warranties of the buyer and its subsidiary have been met; (ii) that all the covenants of the buyer and its subsidiary remain true and correct; (iii) that no orders or decrees exist that prevent the completion of the transaction; and (iv) that buyer and its subsidiary will have delivered specific documents such as employment agreements and officer's certificate.

The buyer generally requires that the following conditions be met prior to or as of the closing date: (i) that all the representations and warranties of the seller remain true and correct; (ii) that all the covenants of the seller have been met; (iii) that no orders or decrees exist that prevent the completion of the transaction; (iv) that seller has secured all necessary consents and waivers; (iv) that seller has secured the release of all liens on its personal or real property; and (v) that seller has delivered specific documents such as the certificate of merger, employee releases, legal counsel's opinion, officer's certificate, and more.

Indemnification

Another common section in most merger and acquisition agreements is the indemnification provision. This may be a stand-alone provision or may be included as a part of the miscellaneous provisions. This section addresses each party's obligations to indemnify the other party. Each deal is unique as to this provision, but one typical type of indemnification protects the buyer from third-party claims and lawsuits against the seller.

Termination

This section appears in every merger and acquisition-related agreement. It may be a stand-alone provision or it may appear as part of the miscellaneous provisions. This section addresses the circumstances that allow for the transaction to be terminated by either side, the effect of a termination, and which party bears the costs and fees associated with a termination.

Miscellaneous Provisions

As with any contract, there is generally a catchall section that discusses all the miscellaneous and relevant provisions that are not included in their own stand-alone sections. Some typical miscellaneous provisions in a merger and acquisition agreement are as follows: (i) that none of the (or only specific) representations, warranties, and covenants survive the closing; (ii) that this agreement represents the entire agreement; (iii) how the parties may amend the agreement; (iv) how the parties must provide notice; (v) the governing law; (vi) dispute resolution; (vii) waiver rights; (viii) that headings are only for descriptive purposes; (ix) that the agreement can be executed in counterparts; (x) that provisions may be severed; (xi) that a jury trial is waived; and more.

Definitions

Depending on the transaction and the length of the agreement, there may or may not be a separate definition section. In some cases, the terms are defined the first time they are used in the agreement and this process is followed throughout. In other cases, there are enough defined terms that it warrants a stand-alone section to make it easier for the readers and users of the agreement. The definition section may be the first section, the last section, or included as an exhibit or appendix to the agreement. If there is not a stand-alone definition section, there is often an index of defined terms and a page cross-reference to where the term is defined or first used.

Exhibits

Most merger and acquisition transactions will contain a number of exhibits that supplement the main agreement. These may be ancillary agreements to the transaction, forms of the certificate of merger, or forms of third party consents. Each deal is unique as to the exhibits that may be attached and made a part of the agreement.

Disclosure Schedules

Many merger and acquisition agreements contain a set of disclosure schedules that list supplemental information noted in the representations and warranties section. Each party to the agreement will have its own set of disclosure schedules that are attached to the final contract. If information is contained in a disclosure schedule, the relevant representation and warranty provision will reference the disclosure schedule. Disclosure schedules are often exceptions to the actual representations and warranties. For instance, a party may stipulate that there is no litigation or no outstanding tax payments owed except as noted in the relevant disclosure schedule. In addition to the exception type disclosure schedule, other disclosure schedules may simply list supplemental information that the parties did not desire to include in the main body of the contract. For example, a party may list all of its benefit plans or insurance policies on the relevant disclosure schedule in conjunction with a representation regarding benefits or insurance.

Ancillary Agreements

In conjunction with the merger and acquisition agreement, there are many ancillary agreements that are prepared and executed as a part of the transaction. These agreements might include the following: (i) promissory note; (ii) third-party consents to the transaction; (iii) employment agreements; (iv) consulting agreements; (v) escrow agreements; (vi) intellectual property assignment; and more. Each transaction is different and so each requires its own set of ancillary documents. However, those listed above are some of the most frequently encountered.

Conclusion

This chapter set forth a brief overview of the main components and most common provisions of a merger and acquisition agreement. In some instances, the merger and acquisition agreement may not contain all of these provisions or such provisions may be titled differently. Additionally, a merger and acquisition agreement will often contain other provisions that were not discussed in this chapter.

CHAPTER 2

BASIC FACT SCENARIO

■ ■ ■

Tree Services, Inc.

Corporate Governance Information

Tree Services, Inc. (TSI) was incorporated in the state of Colorado in January 2003 as a C corporation. TSI has two classes of stock: Common Stock, $0.01 par value (TSI CS) and Preferred Stock, Series A, $5.00 par value (TSI PS). Upon its formation, TSI authorized 1,000,000 shares of TSI CS and 50,000 shares of TSI PS. TSI has not increased the authorized shares for either class of stock since its inception. Pursuant to TSI's bylaws, all matters entitled to be voted on by TSI CS shareholders require a simple majority vote.

Upon its incorporation, TSI issued shares of TSI CS to the three founders as set forth in the table below:

Founder's Name	CS Issued	CS %	Price Paid
Melissa Green	100,000	40%	$10,000
Thomas Shrub	100,000	40%	$10,000
Susan Brown	50,000	20%	$5,000

Each of the founders signed a simple stock purchase agreement with TSI when the TSI CS shares were issued.

To date, TSI has not issued any additional shares of TSI CS. TSI and its outside counsel have discussed the idea of creating a stock option plan for TSI employees. However, the company is only in the beginning stages of this process and has not yet created the stock option plan or finalized any of the details.

While TSI is currently in good financial standing, in early 2005 it was in need of additional capital to grow its business operations and add additional service offerings for its customers. To fund its growth plan, TSI issued 20,000 shares of TSI PS to three investors as set forth in the table below:

Investor's Name	PS Issued	PS %	Price Paid
Erin Mooney	10,000	50%	$50,000
Joe Rosen	5,000	25%	$25,000
Stanley Danger	5,000	25%	$25,000

The TSI PS has a guaranteed dividend payment of $0.25 per share annually and a liquidation preference upon the dissolution or sale of the business (PS Preference). The PS Preference guarantees the TSI PS shareholder the return of his or her initial investment. Each of the investors signed a TSI PS purchase agreement that sets forth these rights.

TSI has three executive officers that are also the original founders of the company. Their pertinent information is set forth in the table below:

Officer's Name	Officer's Position	Officer's Base Salary	Officer's Potential Bonus
Melissa Green	Chief Executive Officer & President	$375,000	$75,000
Thomas Shrub	Chief Financial Officer	$315,000	$60,000
Susan Brown	Senior Vice President & Secretary	$275,000	$25,000

TSI maintains a five-person board of directors. Inside directors (those who are employees of TSI) receive no compensation for their service. Outside directors receive $1,500 for each in-person board meeting attended and $500 for each phone or virtual board meeting attended. In addition to the compensation mentioned above, outside directors are reimbursed for any travel, lodging, and food expenses related to attending in-person board meetings. The information regarding the directors is as follows:

Director's Name	Director's Age	Date Directorship Commenced	Inside/Outside
Melissa Green, Chairperson of the Board	48	January 2, 2003	Inside
Thomas Shrub	49	January 2, 2003	Inside
Jonathon Nixon	44	January 2, 2003	Outside
Erin Mooney	47	January 2, 2005	Outside
Rolland Brown	63	January 2, 2010	Outside

All matters entitled to be voted on by the TSI board of directors require a simple majority vote.

Business Information

Company Overview

TSI is a large local company in the landscaping services industry. The company provides landscape care and maintenance services for both residential and commercial customers. TSI primarily operates in the state of Colorado with some customers in neighboring states. The commercial customers account for approximately 50% of TSI's revenues and the residential customers account for approximately 40%. TSI's remaining revenues come from its winter month service offerings. The company has a total customer base of approximately 200 regular customers and provides services to many one-time customers as well. TSI has a number of large commercial contracts with both private and public parks, golf courses, apartment and condominium complexes, and a few small office parks. Its residential customers range from townhomes and small single-family homes to large single-family and mountain homes.

Company Services

TSI's primary focus is on the care and maintenance of trees, but it also offers other related landscaping services to a lesser extent. TSI offers the following tree services: tree pruning, tree removal, emergency tree care, branch removal around utility lines, and other related services such as fertilization, cabling and bracing, and insect and disease control. TSI also provides landscape maintenance services such as leaf clearing, lawn mowing and care, basic irrigation systems, and pest control. During the winter months, TSI offers snow removal and holiday light hanging services.

Company Equipment and Fleet

TSI maintains an average fleet of 13–15 trucks and trailers, including tree trucks with chippers and grapples, tree trucks with aerial lifters, site trucks, trucks with snow removal plows, and spray, fertilizer, and injection trucks. In addition to its trucks and trailers, TSI also maintains a number of hydraulic truck cranes, stump and limb grinders, stump removers, brush chippers, chain saws, clippers, snow blowers, and other related tools.

Company Staffing

TSI employs 70 crew workers, two arborists, five office staff, and the three company founders. Of the 70 crew workers, approximately 35–45 are seasonal employees who work for TSI only during the months of March–November, which are typically TSI's busiest months. The remaining 25–35 crew workers are employed by TSI year-round. Of the year-round crew workers, ten are crew leaders and supervisors.

Financial Information

High-level TSI financial information for the current fiscal year (projected) and past two fiscal years is set forth in the table below:

	Current FY Ending December 31 (Projected)	FY Ended December 31 (One Year Prior)	FY Ended December 31 (Two Years Prior)
Total Assets	$18,000,000	$15,600,000	$13,900,000
Total Liabilities	$11,250,000	$10,000,000	$9,000,000
Long-Term Debt (included in total liabilities above)	$1,875,000	$1,950,000	$2,000,000
Total Revenue	$34,650,000	$31,500,000	$30,000,000
EBITDA	$4,500,000	$4,000,000	$3,600,000
Net Income	$1,525,000	$1,250,000	$1,100,000

Dutch Elm Company

Corporate Governance Information

Dutch Elm Company (DEC) was incorporated in the state of Nevada in January 1995 as a C corporation. DEC has one class of stock: Common Stock, $0.01 par value (DEC CS). Upon its formation, DEC authorized 5,000,000 shares of DEC CS. DEC has not increased the authorized shares of DEC CS since its inception. All matters entitled to be voted on by the DEC CS shareholders require a simple majority vote.

Upon its incorporation in 1995, DEC issued 500,000 shares of DEC CS to the three founders as set forth in the table below:

Founder's Name	CS Issued	CS %	Price Paid
Fred Wilcox	225,000	45%	$157,500
Bernard Thompson	150,000	30%	$105,000
Margaret Fife	125,000	25%	$87,500

Each of the founders signed a simple stock purchase agreement with DEC when the shares were issued.

DEC has issued shares of DEC CS in addition to the stock held by the founders. DEC has a stock option plan in place for its full-time employees. DEC can issue up to 100,000 DEC CS options pursuant to the stock option plan. To date, DEC has issued 25,000 DEC CS options. Each option is worth one share of DEC CS upon exercise. Of the 25,000 options issued, 10,000 options have been exercised with the resulting shares of DEC CS issued to employees.

DEC has five executive officers, three of whom are also the original founders of the company. Their pertinent information is set forth in the table below:

Officer's Name	Officer's Position	Officer's Base Salary	Officer's Potential Bonus
Fred Wilcox	Chief Executive Officer & President	$550,000	$120,000
Bernard Thompson	Chief Operating Officer	$525,000	$60,000
Margaret Fife	Chief Financial Officer	$525,000	$60,000
Michelle Smith	Senior Vice President of Sales & Marketing	$475,000	$40,000
Robert Lawson	Vice President & Secretary	$415,000	$15,000

In 2000, DEC sold 300,000 additional shares of DEC CS for $750,000 to a small venture capital firm, FS Capital. DEC used the funds from this sale to grow the business, expand its service offerings, and purchase additional equipment. FS Capital signed a stock purchase agreement with DEC as a part of the sale. The FS Capital stock purchase agreement provided FS Capital with ability to name two persons to the DEC board of directors until such time as DEC either re-purchases the FS Capital DEC CS shares or DEC repays FS Capital two times the amount of its original investment through DEC dividend payments. To date, DEC has not fulfilled either of these requirements and as a result, FS Capital still has two seats on the DEC board of directors.

DEC maintains a seven-person board of directors. Inside directors (those employed by the company) receive no compensation for their service. Each outside director receives $2,500 for each in-person board meeting attended and $1,000 for each phone or virtual board meeting attended. In addition, outside directors are reimbursed for any travel, lodging, and food expenses related to attending in-person meetings. The director's information is as follows:

Director's Name	Director's Age	Date Directorship Commenced	Inside/Outside
Fred Wilcox, Chairperson of the Board	55	January 2, 1995	Inside
Bernard Thompson	58	January 2, 1995	Inside
Margaret Fife	46	January 2, 1995	Inside
William Carlton	65	January 2, 1998	Outside
Lisa Montgomery	51	January 2, 1999	Outside
Harold Jenson (FS Capital appointee)	43	January 2, 2000	Outside
Susan Watertown (FS Capital appointee)	34	January 2, 2000	Outside

All matters entitled to be voted on by the DEC board of directors require a simple majority vote.

Business Information

Company Overview

DEC is a national company in the landscaping services industry. DEC provides tree care and maintenance, and landscape care and maintenance services for both residential and commercial customers throughout the continental United States. The company has a customer base of over 1,500 regular customers, as well as thousands of one-time customers. DEC's commercial customers account for approximately 50% of its revenues and residential customers account for approximately 45%. DEC's remaining revenues come from its winter month service offerings. DEC has many local and large national commercial contracts with private and public parks, private and public golf courses, apartment and condominium complexes, planned communities, small and large office parks, and small ski resorts. Its residential customers range from townhomes and small single-family homes to large single-family and vacation homes.

Company Services

DEC provides all types of horticultural services including a broad array of tree-related and landscaping services. It also works with a number of utility companies to clear tree growth from power lines. DEC's tree-related service offerings include: pruning, removal, emergency tree care, surgery, spraying, clearing around utility lines, cabling and bracing, watering, and fertilization. Additionally, DEC provides a wide array of landscaping services including construction and design, leaf clearing, lawn mowing and care, small and large irrigation systems, and disease and pest control. During the winter months, DEC provides snow removal to all of its customers, as well as winter landscape maintenance services. In addition, in severe storm conditions, DEC may assist small towns and cities with snow removal.

Company Equipment and Fleet

In order to meet the needs of its commercial and residential customers, DEC maintains a large fleet of trucks and trailers, including tree trucks with chippers and grapples, tree trucks with aerial lifters, site trucks, trucks with snow removal plows, and spray, fertilizer and injection trucks. In addition to its trucks and trailers, DEC also maintains a number of hydraulic truck cranes, stump and limb grinders, stump removers, brush chippers, chain saws, clippers, snow blowers, and other related tools.

Company Staffing

DEC employs more than 400 crew workers and one to two arborists for each geographical region it serves. Approximately 50% of its crew workers are seasonal employees who work for DEC only during the months of March-November. DEC's corporate headquarters are located in Las Vegas, Nevada where it employs a staff of 60 full-time employees to oversee and run its national operations.

Financial Information

High level DEC financial information for the current fiscal year (projected) and past two fiscal years is set forth in the table below:

	Current FY Ending December 31 (Projected)	FY Ended December 31 (One Year Prior)	FY Ended December 31 (Two Years Prior)
Total Assets	$109,000,000	$100,000,000	$92,000,000
Total Liabilities	$70,300,000	$67,000,000	$63,500,000
Long-Term Debt (included in total liabilities above)	$8,200,000	$6,900,000	$5,800,000
Total Revenue	$225,000,000	$213,000,000	$192,000,000
EBITDA	$24,750,000	$21,500,000	$19,200,000
Net Income	$7,750,000	$6,200,000	$4,400,000

CHAPTER 3

ATTORNEY-CLIENT
ENGAGEMENT LETTER

■ ■ ■

Brief Introduction to Attorney-Client Engagement Letters

Once the attorney has determined that she desires to represent the client in the transaction, the attorney and the client should enter into an attorney-client engagement letter. The engagement letter may also be referred to as a retainer agreement or fee agreement. The attorney-client engagement letter sets forth the relationship between the parties. Some of the most crucial aspects of the attorney-client engagement letter include (i) identification of the client; (ii) the scope of the representation; (iii) the payment of the retainer, if applicable; (iv) fees, and expenses; (v) obligations of the parties regarding communication and cooperation; (vi) handling of disputes; (vii) termination or withdrawal; and more. Many states require that an attorney-client engagement letter be in place and that it specifically set forth the manner in which fees will be billed to the client.

Part 1: Attorney-Client Engagement Letter Drafting Assignment

You are a junior associate at William & Bowers, PC and the senior partner at the firm, Bryan Williams, that Ms. Green, Mr. Shrub, and Ms. Brown (the "TSI Executives") spoke with has asked you to work with the lead attorney, Lisa Goodman, on this representation. An initial client meeting is scheduled for three weeks from today. Mr. Williams has asked that you prepare the Attorney-Client Engagement Letter (Letter) for this matter based on the applicable laws of your state. Mr. Williams has stated that he wants TSI to pay an initial retainer in the amount of $20,000 for this matter due within five business days after execution of the Letter by both parties. He does not have an estimate of potential fees for the engagement at this point in time.

Mr. Williams would like to review the Letter before it is forwarded to TSI Executives for their review and execution on behalf of TSI. He wants to forward the Letter to them at least one week prior to the initial client meeting. Mr. Williams has asked that you submit the draft Letter via email to his and Ms. Goodman's attention.

Part 2: Additional Facts for the Assignment

Williams & Bowers, PC is located in Denver, Colorado and is a boutique firm that specializes in all types of transactional law, from contract drafting and negotiation to mergers and acquisitions to capital raises. Williams & Bowers, PC has four partners and 11 associates. In addition, the firm has two certified paralegals, three legal assistants, one law clerk, and an office administrator.

The TSI Executives, who are the founders and sole common stock shareholders of TSI have retained your firm, Williams & Bowers, PC, to assist with a potential sale of their landscaping business through some type of merger transaction. None of the TSI Executives have worked with your firm in the past, but after an initial phone consultation with Mr. Williams, the TSI Executives made the decision to hire the firm. Mr. Williams accepted the representation of TSI on behalf of Williams & Bowers.

The TSI Executives informed Mr. Williams that Ms. Green has had informal conversations with Fred Wilcox, the Chief Executive Officer of DEC regarding the potential sale of TSI to DEC. Ms. Green and Mr. Wilcox have only engaged in preliminary discussions to date and no final decisions have been made regarding the actual sale of TSI to DEC or any potential structure of this business transaction. Further, the parties have not entered into a letter of intent or any other legally binding agreement or documents.

The TSI Executives anticipate using your firm for all aspects of the potential sale of TSI to DEC, including reviewing TSI's current corporate structure and governance documents; assisting in the potential due diligence request and investigation by DEC; assisting in negotiating the deal terms; drafting, reviewing, and negotiating the merger and acquisition agreement; drafting, reviewing, and negotiating all relevant ancillary documents such as the confidentiality agreement, letter of intent, employment agreements, etc.; preparing any necessary corporate documents to effectuate the potential transaction, including third party consents, contract assignments, and shareholder and director resolutions; and issuing a legal opinion, if one is requested by DEC and its counsel. Mr. Williams does not expect that Williams & Bowers will be involved in any litigation, including arbitration, administrative hearings, or court proceedings related to this representation. These particular services, if necessary, may be added at a later point in time by a separate agreement signed by the parties at the then-prevailing rates. The details regarding your firm and the current applicable billing rates and fees are set forth below:

Williams & Bowers, PC
2200 Thirtieth Avenue
Suite 8900
Denver, CO 80202
www.wblaw.com
Phone: (720) 555-5555
Facsimile: (720) 555-5556

Billing Rate or Item Charge	Rate/Charge
Partner Billing Rates	$325–$385/hour
Senior Associate Billing Rates	$225–$275/hour
Junior Associate Billing Rates	$135–$185/hour
Paralegal Billing Rates	$65–$85/hour
Law Clerk Billing Rates	$45–$60/hour
Database Research Charges (e.g. Westlaw)	Actual Cost
Long-Distance Telephone Charges	No Cost/Charge
Photocopy & Printing Charges	No Cost/Charge

<u>Further Billing Information</u>: The firm bills in six-minute increments and it is anticipated that billing rates may increase in the future. Billable hours include preparation, research, and client-related travel time. The firm also bills for other reasonable costs and expenses. The firm bills its clients once per month. Any payments owed to the firm must be paid within fifteen calendar days of the date of each invoice or interest will accrue at the rate of 12% per annum on the unpaid balance.

Part 3: Useful Resources for Students

American Bar Association, *Engagement Letter Checklist*, 35 No. 7 Law Prac. 49 (November/December 2009).

Chapter 30. Attorneys at Law—Letter of Engagement, 3 Am. Jur. Legal Forms 2d § 30:6 (2014).

Attorney-Client Relationships: Attorney Duties and Engagement Letters, 2010 No. 9 Business Counselor Update 2 (Sept. 2010).

Nancy J. Geenen, *A Well-Crafted Engagement Letter Saves Trouble Down the Line*, 95–DEC A.B.A. J. 50 (Dec. 2009).

Luther T. Munford, *Your Client's First Impression: Drafting Engagement Letters*, 53 No. 2 DRI For Def. 70 (Feb. 2011).

John M. Palmeri and Franz Hardy, *Getting Hitched: Confirming the Attorney/Client Engagement*, 32–JAN Colo. Law. 37 (Jan. 2013).

Ch. 2—The Client-Lawyer Relationship, Restatement (Third) Law Governing Lawyers, §§ 14–33 (2000).

CHAPTER 4

CONFIDENTIALITY AGREEMENT

■ ■ ■

Brief Introduction to Confidentiality Agreements

Prior to commencing full-blown negotiations of a merger and acquisition and sharing information regarding their respective entities, the parties to the transaction should enter into a confidentiality agreement. This agreement may be unilateral or mutual depending upon whether only one party or both parties will share confidential information with the other. The confidentiality agreement allows the parties to share sensitive information with each other, while restricting the parties from sharing that same information with non-affiliated third parties or using that information for a purpose other than the merger negotiations and transaction. By entering into this agreement, the non-breaching party may seek damages in the event of a breach or release of confidential information by the other party.

Part 1: Confidentiality Agreement Drafting Assignment

You are a junior associate at Williams & Bowers, PC, TSI's outside counsel. Lisa Goodman, the senior attorney handling the TSI transaction, has asked you to draft the confidentiality agreement. Ms. Goodman desires a standard unilateral confidentiality agreement meaning that only TSI will be sharing information with DEC. She has also requested that it be TSI friendly.

Lisa Goodman wants to review the confidentiality agreement before it is forwarded to the TSI Executives for their review and execution on behalf of TSI. She has asked that you submit the draft confidentiality agreement to her for her review.

Part 2: Additional Facts for the Assignment

Ms. Goodman stated that the following additional information should be taken into account when drafting the confidentiality agreement:

- The TSI Executives have executed the Attorney-Client Engagement Letter and retained Williams & Bowers, PC. They have also confirmed with Bryan Williams that they intend to move forward with the potential sale of the business to DEC. Before they begin the process of sharing

information with DEC, they want a confidentiality agreement in place.

- The TSI Executives feel strongly about protecting TSI's business information and employees. As a result, TSI wants the information provided to DEC, whether through the due diligence process or otherwise, to remain confidential.

- TSI and the TSI Executives believe the parties can reach an agreement and close the transaction within 6–12 months of starting discussions and so consider a term of one year for the confidentiality agreement sufficient.

- TSI and the TSI Executives do not want to run the risk of losing any of the TSI employees as a result of this process and desire a non-solicitation provision in the confidentiality agreement that is in effect during the term of the confidentiality agreement and for 18 months after termination or expiration of the agreement.

- The TSI Executives know that DEC does not want them to solicit or talk to other potential buyers of TSI during the term of the confidentiality agreement and the TSI Executives are willing to agree to those terms. However, if the confidentiality agreement expires or is terminated, TSI and the TSI Executives want to be able to immediately contact other potential buyers of TSI.

- The TSI Executives desire to have Colorado law govern so that any contractual issues or disputes are resolved in their home state.

- The TSI Executives do not want the due diligence process to consume the time of all of TSI's employees and so they have designated select parties that DEC and its counsel can contact directly for informational requests. Those parties are as follows:

Melissa Green	Chief Executive Officer & President
Thomas Shrub	Chief Financial Officer
Michael Lewis	Senior Vice President of Finance
Margaret Smith	Dunton & Teller, LLC, TSI's Public Accountants/Auditors

- TSI and the TSI Executives have also requested that DEC share the information with as few people as possible and that anyone who has access to confidential information be covered under the confidentiality

agreement. Some of the additional relevant parties associated with DEC are as follows:

Jeffrey McClelland, Partner	McClelland, Springer & Henderson, LLC, DEC's Outside Counsel
Maria Snyder	Pierce & Conway, LLC, DEC's Public Accountants/Auditors
Richard Clark	Northern Bank

Part 3: Useful Resources for Students

L. M. Brownlee, *Chapter 1. Intellectual Property Due Diligence: Preliminary Considerations*, IP Due Diligence in Corp. Trans. §§ 1:30 & 1:33 (last updated Apr. 2014).

Eduardo Gallardo, Robert Litle, & Travis Souza, *M&A Confidentiality Agreements—Recent Guidance From Delaware*, 16 No. 6 M & A Law. 1 (June 2012).

Chapter 12. The Exchange of Confidential Information in Negotiated Acquisitions—Confidentiality Agreements—Provisions—Restrictions on Use, 1 Corp. Couns. Gd. Acq. & Divest. §§ 12:1–3, (last updated Mar. 2014).

Chapter 1. How to Formulate a Single-Step Acquisitions Strategy—Confidentiality Agreements, Corporate Acquisitions §§ 1:29–1:30 (last updated Apr. 2014).

Chapter 1. Introduction to Acquisitions and Divestitures—The Documents—Common Documents—Confidentiality Agreements, 1 Corp. Couns. Gd. Acq. & Divest. § 1:49 (last updated Mar. 2014).

CHAPTER 5

LETTER OF INTENT

■ ■ ■

Brief Introduction to the Letter of Intent

The letter of intent is an agreement between the parties contemplating an acquisition that sets forth the major terms of the proposed transaction. The letter of intent is generally a non-binding agreement meaning that while it includes the important terms regarding the proposed merger and acquisition, it does not obligate the parties to consummate the transaction. The buyer and seller enter into a letter of intent to signify their desire to move forward with the proposed transaction and often use this agreement to avoid any potential misunderstandings as to the terms of the deal.

Part 1: Letter of Intent Drafting Assignment

You are a junior associate at McClelland, Springer & Henderson, LLC, DEC's outside counsel. Mr. McClelland, the partner overseeing DEC's acquisition of TSI, has asked the team on this deal to draft the letter of intent that sets forth the preliminary details of the acquisition. Melina Chang, the senior attorney, has assigned this task to you. Ms. Chang has asked you to prepare a draft of the letter of intent for her review.

(Students should follow their professor's direction as to whether to utilize the facts and terms presented below in Part 2 of this chapter or the negotiated terms established from the supplemental class exercise to draft the letter of intent.)

Part 2: Additional Facts for the Assignment

The final draft of the confidentiality agreement between DEC and TSI has been circulated to both parties and is currently being finalized. DEC and TSI would both like to establish the basic terms of the proposed acquisition and desire that a letter of intent be drafted. DEC is taking the lead on the letter of intent.

Ms. Chang has provided you with the following additional information to assist in drafting the letter of intent:

- DEC and TSI have had multiple conversations regarding the purchase price and are close to a final agreement on that front. DEC would like to include that figure in the initial draft of the letter of intent. The tentative purchase price is the equivalent of $7,500,000.

- DEC will pay the purchase price through a combination of cash and DEC common stock (DEC CS). DEC intends to pay 75% of the purchase price in cash at closing ($5,625,000) and pay the remaining amount in the form of DEC CS at closing ($1,875,000 worth).

- The DEC CS will be valued two business days prior to closing in order to determine the number of shares to be issued to the TSI common stockholders.

- The payment to each TSI common stockholder will be made in accordance with the percentage that each common stockholder of TSI owns on the business day immediately preceding closing.

- DEC will create a new wholly-owned Nevada subsidiary, TSI NEWCO, Inc. and will merge TSI with and into that new subsidiary at closing.

- While DEC will buy all of the TSI common stock and assume the assets and liabilities of TSI, DEC has requested that a few specific items be carved out from the purchase. DEC will not assume the following obligations:

  o TSI workers' compensation claims based on injuries that occurred prior to the closing date.

  o TSI's revolving line of credit and security agreement with Big Bank in the amount of $750,000 ($225,000 outstanding and unpaid).

- DEC has committed to retaining all three of the TSI Executives in some capacity. Each of these persons will be required to enter into and execute a new employment or consulting agreement with DEC at the closing, each may receive an increase over their current annual TSI salary, and each may be eligible for other perquisites dependent upon the capacity in which each is retained by DEC.

- DEC would also like the option to selectively hire individual TSI employees, though at this point in time DEC has not identified which TSI employees it would like to hire and at what compensation level. After DEC identifies these employees, each employee will be required to submit an employment application to DEC and go through an interview process.

- Both DEC and TSI have agreed to the following timeline for the acquisition:

- All due diligence materials will be exchanged on or before five business days after execution of the letter of intent.

- The due diligence review will be completed on or before 35 calendar days after execution of the letter of intent.

- DEC's counsel will prepare the initial draft of the merger and acquisition agreement and will circulate the initial draft within 15 calendar days after execution of the letter of intent.

- The parties have agreed that closing must occur within 270 days after execution of the letter of intent or either party can terminate the letter of intent without further obligation.

- DEC requires that TSI deal with DEC exclusively until such time as the merger is complete or the letter of intent is terminated.

- TSI must continue to operate its business in the ordinary course.

- The parties have agreed to pay their own legal expenses in regard to the potential acquisition.

- The letter of intent should provide that:

  - Each party has typical termination rights.

  - That neither party will make a public announcement without the approval of the other party.

  - Any other appropriate miscellaneous provisions.

Part 3: Useful Resources for Students

Part H. Expansion and Contraction. Chapter 19. Mergers & Acquisitions—The Use of the Letter of Intent in M&A Transactions, Mod. Corp. Checklists § 19:23 (last updated May 2014).

Chapter 9 Corporate Counsel's Guide to Letters of Intent—Appendix 9–A. Checklist for Drafting Letters of Intent, 1 Corp. Couns. Gd. to Acq. & Divest. Appendix 9–A (last updated Mar. 2014).

Chapter 2. Checklist for Drafting Letters of Intent—Introduction, Sp. Study for Corp. Couns. on Using Letters of Intent in Bus. Trans. § 2:1 (last updated Aug. 2013).

Simon M. Lorne & Joy Marlene Bryan, *Chapter 3. Negotiated Acquisition Transactions—Letter of Intent,* 11 Acquisitions & Mergers § 3:54 (last updated Jun. 2014).

CHAPTER 6

DUE DILIGENCE MEMORANDUM

■ ■ ■

Brief Introduction to the Due Diligence Memorandum

When the buyer and seller have reached the stage in the merger and acquisition process where both parties are in a position to commit to moving forward with the transaction and desire to do so, the due diligence process generally begins. Due diligence is the process that the buyer undertakes to investigate and understand the company and the business it is acquiring. While one component of due diligence is identifying and assessing legal risks and business concerns, the process also enables the buyer to learn more about the potential opportunities that may result from the acquisition.

Due diligence is typically an on-going investigative process and not a one shot undertaking. While it is often commenced early in the transaction, it is not unusual for drafting of the merger and acquisition agreement to be under way while the due diligence process continues. It is the buyer's goal to learn as much as it can about the business and the company it is acquiring. The depth and length of due diligence is driven by the type of deal, the size of the deal, and the overall timetable for the deal. No two due diligence processes unfold the same way, as each is unique to the specific circumstances of that merger and acquisition.

Part 1: Due Diligence Memorandum Drafting Assignment

The partner in charge of DEC's due diligence process at McClelland, Springer & Henderson, LLC, Zoie Springer, has asked you to participate as a member of the team that will undertake the due diligence investigation of TSI.

You have been asked to review the five contracts listed and discussed below. Your assignment is to draft a due diligence memorandum regarding your findings. You should draft your due diligence memo as if it was a stand-alone document that ultimately will be provided to DEC. At a minimum, you should include the following sections in your due diligence memo: (i) Introduction and Overview; (ii) Detailed Contract Review; (iii) Next Steps, and Additional Actions or Requests; and (iv) Conclusion.

The five contracts for your review (*included in Appendix B*) are as follows:

1. Commercial Lease Agreement between Tree Services, Inc. and Giant Real Estate Company (Lease Agreement).

    a. This lease is for TSI's main facility in the state of Colorado.

    b. DEC would like to assume the Lease Agreement and continue operating from the facility under the same terms after the acquisition is complete.

2. Revolving Line of Credit and Security Agreement between Tree Services, Inc. and Big Bank (LOC).

    a. TSI uses the LOC to purchase equipment as needed to run the day-to-day operations of its business.

    b. Big Bank has filed a UCC financing statement encumbering TSI's equipment as collateral for the LOC.

    c. DEC will require TSI to pay off the LOC on the closing date of the transaction with proceeds from the acquisition. DEC plans to require a provision in the acquisition agreement that, at closing, it will wire payment proceeds directly to Big Bank to pay off the outstanding balance on the LOC. The remaining proceeds will be distributed pursuant to the merger and acquisition agreement.

3. Website Development and Maintenance Agreement between Tree Services, Inc. and Webmasters Limited (Website Agreement).

    a. DEC desires to maintain the existing TSI website after the closing of the transaction.

    b. DEC has indicated that it will make a decision on whether to retain Webmasters Limited to manage, update, and oversee the TSI website and whether to assume the Website Agreement based upon the due diligence investigation.

4. Executive Employment Agreement between Tree Services, Inc. and Melissa Green (Employment Agreement).

    a. DEC desires to retain Melissa Green in some capacity after the closing of the transaction.

    b. DEC has indicated that it may be willing to amend the current Employment Agreement or may require Ms. Green to execute a new employment agreement.

    c. DEC has indicated that if the current Employment Agreement is too onerous based on the due diligence investigation, then it will require a new employment agreement with Ms. Green.

  5. Form Services Agreement between Tree Services, Inc. and its customers (Form Services Agreement).

    a. TSI utilizes this Form Services Agreement for most service contracts with its customers.

    b. DEC will assume almost all of TSI's current customers under the then in-effect Form Services Agreement.

    c. DEC will move TSI customers to the DEC services agreement as they renew their contract.

Part 2: Additional Facts for the Assignment

You are a junior associate at the firm and this is the first time you have worked as a member of a due diligence team for any type of transaction.

Ms. Springer has indicated to you that she prefers you err on the side of including too much information in your due diligence memo as opposed to omitting any potentially important information. Ms. Springer has also indicated that she expects you to offer enough information regarding the pros and cons of assuming the Lease Agreement and Employment Agreement, and of continuing to use Webmasters Limited for the maintenance, updating, and upkeep of the existing TSI website so that DEC can make an informed decision about how to handle those contracts.

While you are only reviewing a select number of agreements that would be part of the overall due diligence process, Ms. Springer has requested that you draft your memo as if it was a stand-alone due diligence memo.

Part 3: Useful Resources for Students

Due Diligence Reviews in Mergers and Acquisitions, 24 No. 3 Corp. Couns. Quarterly ART 7 (July 2008).

Michael S. Dorf, *Evolving Due Diligence Strategies for Buyers and Sellers In M&A Transactions,* Business Due Diligence Strategies, 2011 WL 2115898 (May 2011).

Chapter 3 Comprehensive Checklist: Considerations in an Acquisition or Divestiture—Due Diligence, 1 Corp. Couns. Gd. to Acq. & Divest. § 3:8 (last updated Mar. 2014).

Part H. Expansion and Contraction, Chapter 19. Mergers and Acquisitions—Conducting Due Diligence in M&A Transactions, Mod. Corp. Checklists § 19:22 (last updated Mar. 2014).

Mark H. Davis, *Adding Value While Minimizing Risk In The M&A Due Diligence Process*, 2012 WL 1188214 (May 2012).

CHAPTER 7

THE MERGER

■ ■ ■

Brief Introduction to the Merger Section

The merger section of a merger and acquisition agreement sets forth a number of critical details regarding the transaction. The first thing this section should address is how the merger will be structured or in other words it should describe whether it will be a statutory merger, a straight forward or reverse merger, or a triangular forward or reverse merger. This information indicates how the entities will be owned and operated after closing takes place and also indicates which entities will continue to exist and survive post-closing.

The merger section contains relevant information regarding logistics of the transaction. It generally sets out the effective date and time of the merger, as well as the location and date of the closing of the merger. This provision should also indicate the documents to be filed with the various offices of the Secretary of State to officially effectuate the merger and the time frame in which those documents must be filed.

The merger section should also include a provision that discusses the effects of the merger on the entities involved in the transaction, such as future ownership, control, and other significant operational changes. Lastly, the merger section should contain provisions that set forth how the articles or certificate of incorporation and bylaws of the various entities will be treated (stay the same, be restated, or be amended). It should also address who will be the officers and directors of the new subsidiary or surviving entity and whether these will be initial officers and directors until others can be qualified and appointed or if they will be the continuing officers and directors.

It is not unusual to see the merger section and the merger consideration section (discussed in Chapter 8) of the merger and acquisition agreement combined into one main article or section of the agreement.

Part 1: The Merger Section Drafting Assignment

You are a junior associate at McClelland, Springer & Henderson, LLC, DEC's outside counsel. The firm will be taking the lead in drafting the merger and acquisition agreement. Melina Chang, the senior associate overseeing the transaction for DEC, has asked you to draft the "merger section" of the acquisition agreement. She has requested that you submit a final draft to her attention so that she can review it and provide you with comments and feedback.

Part 2: Additional Facts for the Assignment

In order to prepare the merger section, Ms. Chang provided you with the following additional information:

- DEC will create a wholly owned subsidiary named "TSI NEWCO, Inc." (TSINI) prior to the closing.
- TSINI will be incorporated in the State of Nevada.
- DEC will be the sole shareholder of TSINI.
- The current officers of DEC will be appointed as the officers of TSINI until such time as new officers can be qualified and appointed.
- The current officers of DEC also will be appointed as the directors of TSINI until such time as new directors can be qualified and appointed.
- TSI will be merged with and into TSINI at closing and TSINI will be the surviving entity.
- DEC will rename TSINI on or before five business days after the effective date of the merger and the new name of the surviving entity will be Tree Services, Inc., a Nevada corporation.
- The closing will take place 75 days from today's date at the corporate offices of DEC in Las Vegas, Nevada.
- The effective date of the merger shall be the date the certificate of merger is filed with the appropriate Secretary of State or another date agreed upon by all of the parties to the transaction.
- The current articles of incorporation and bylaws of TSINI will be restated and adopted as the articles and bylaws of TSINI at closing.

Part 3: Useful Resources for Students

50 State Regulatory Surveys: Business Organizations: Corporations, *Corporate Mergers, Acquisitions, Liquidations, and Dissolutions*, Thomson Reuters (June 2013).

Alan S. Gutterman, *Part II. Formation and Operation of Business Entities, Chapter 80. Conversion and Other Entity Form Changes—Merger*, 6 Business Transactions Solutions § 80:131 (last updated Jun. 2014).

Alan S. Gutterman, *Part X. Acquisitions and Divestitures, Chapter 297. Corporate Mergers—Types of Mergers*, 29 Business Transactions Solutions § 297:4 (last updated Jun. 2014).

E. Thom Rumberger, Jr, *Chapter 5. Structuring the M&A Exit Transaction*, The Acquisition and Sale of Emerging Growth Companies: The M&A Exit (2d ed.), §§ 5:20–5:25 (last updated May 2009).

Alan S. Gutterman, *Part X. Acquisitions and Divestitures, Chapter 291. Buying and Selling Businesses—Corporations—Mergers*, 26 Business Transactions Solutions § 291:71 (last updated Jun. 2014).

Alan S. Gutterman, *Part X. Acquisitions and Divestitures, Chapter 297. Corporate Mergers*, 29 Business Transactions Solutions §§ 297:26–297:27 (last updated Jun. 2014).

Jeffrey Manns, *The Merger Agreement Myth*, 98 Cornell L. Rev. 1143 (July, 2013).

CHAPTER 8

MERGER CONSIDERATION

■ ■ ■

Brief Introduction to the Merger Consideration Section

The merger consideration section of a merger and acquisition agreement sets forth the details regarding the consideration the buyer will issue or pay to the seller. The merger consideration is unique to each transaction, as the payment terms of the transaction will dictate what must be included in this section. In some cases, it may be a straight cash deal or it may be a straight conversion of the seller's stock for the buyer's stock. In other instances, it may be a combination of cash, stock, promissory notes, or other cash equivalents. No matter the structure of the consideration, the merger consideration section should accurately reflect the transaction in as much as detail as necessary.

In the case of a straight cash or cash equivalent deal, this section would reflect the amount of cash and cash equivalents to be paid by the buyer to the seller, including such details as the amount of cash consideration, the amount of cash equivalent consideration, how and when the cash and cash equivalent consideration will be paid, if any amount of the cash consideration will be held back for payment post-closing and upon what terms, and other relevant information.

In the case of a conversion of the seller's stock for the buyer's stock, this section would reflect such details as the conversion ratio, how fractional shares will be handled, what will happen with stock options and treasury stock, if any exist, how preferred stock will be handled, if any exists, how the exchange of the shares will take place, how lost certificates will be managed, how dissenting shares will be handled, and more.

It is not unusual to see the merger consideration and the merger section (discussed in Chapter 7) of the merger and acquisition agreement combined into one main article or section.

Part 1: The Merger Section Drafting Assignment

You are a junior associate at McClelland, Springer & Henderson, LLC, DEC's outside counsel. The firm will be taking the lead in drafting the merger and acquisition agreement. Melina Chang, the senior associate overseeing the transaction, has asked you to draft the "merger

37

consideration" section of the contract. She has requested that you submit a final draft to her attention so that she can review it and provide you with comments and feedback.

Part 2: Additional Facts for the Assignment

In order to prepare the merger consideration section, Ms. Chang provided you with the following additional information:

- DEC will create a wholly owned subsidiary named "TSI NEWCO, Inc." (TSINI) prior to the closing.
- TSINI will be incorporated in the State of Nevada.
- DEC will be the sole shareholder of TSINI.
- None of the common or preferred shareholders of TSI are dissenting to the transaction and so there are no dissenter's rights.

Common Stockholders Merger Consideration

DEC shall pay the following consideration to the TSI common stock shareholders based on their TSI percentage ownership interests in exchange for 100% of their TSI common stock shares:

- $5,625,000 cash at closing:
  - $4,837,500 of the cash consideration will be paid to the TSI common stock shareholders on the closing date.
  - $225,000 of the cash consideration will be paid directly to Big Bank on the closing date to satisfy TSI's outstanding balance on its revolving line of credit.
  - $562,500 of the cash consideration shall be placed in an escrow account and shall be released to the common stockholders of TSI no later than the one-year anniversary of the closing or the date any outstanding litigation claims against TSI existing as of the closing date have been dismissed or settled in full.
- $1,875,000 worth of shares of DEC common stock. DEC's common stock is currently valued at $20.00 per share.
- In exchange for the consideration, the TSI common stock shareholders will surrender 100% of their TSI common shares.

Preferred Stockholders Merger Consideration

DEC shall pay the following consideration to the TSI preferred stockholders at closing in exchange for the redemption and cancellation of the TSI preferred shares:

- DEC shall pay the liquidation preference, which is 1.0X the amount of the preferred stockholder's original investment.

- DEC shall pay the guaranteed dividend payment of $0.25 per share that would have been due at the end of TSI's current fiscal year.

Part 3: Useful Resources for Students

Alan S. Gutterman, *Part X. Acquisitions and Divestitures, Chapter 297. Corporate Mergers—Drafting Checklist*, 29 Business Transactions Solutions § 297:160 (last updated Jun. 2014).

Alan S. Gutterman, *Part X. Acquisitions and Divestitures, Chapter 297. Corporate Mergers—Consideration and Payment*, 29 Business Transactions Solutions § 297:11 (last updated Jun. 2014).

50 State Regulatory Surveys: Business Organizations: Corporations, *Corporate Mergers, Acquisitions, Liquidations, and Dissolutions*, Thomson Reuters (June 2013).

Jeffrey Manns, *The Merger Agreement Myth*, 98 Cornell L. Rev. 1143 (July, 2013).

CHAPTER 9

REPRESENTATIONS AND WARRANTIES

■ ■ ■

Brief Introduction to Representations and Warranties

Representations and warranties are statements that a party sets forth in the merger and acquisition agreement that pertain to its business, assets, liabilities, and other related matters. In essence, representations and warranties are disclosures regarding various matters that act to allocate potential risks among the parties. In addition to allocating risk, representations and warranties also provide a party with the ability to terminate the agreement or to seek indemnification for certain matters. Many representations and warranties are supplemented by a disclosure schedule that is attached to the agreement as an appendix. The disclosure schedule may list specific items referenced in the representation and warranty—such as a list of all intellectual property owned. In the alternative, the disclosure schedule may list exceptions or carve-outs to the representation and warranty—such as a list of pending litigation.

The selling company is the party that provides the majority of the representations and warranties, though the selling shareholders, if applicable, are also generally asked to make certain representations and warranties regarding the shares they own and are selling. In addition, the buyer and its merger subsidiary, if one exists, may also make representations and warranties though these are generally less extensive than the ones made by and expected of the seller.

Part 1: Seller's Representations and Warranties Drafting Assignment

Melina Chang, the senior associate in charge of DEC's acquisition of TSI, has asked you to participate on the team that is drafting the TSI representations and warranties section of the merger and acquisition agreement. In particular, you have been tasked with drafting the following TSI representations and warranties, including the preparation of any relevant disclosure schedules: Authority and No Conflict; Authorized Capital; Compliance with Legal Requirements and Governmental Authorizations; Legal Proceedings; Intellectual Property; and Contracts.

Ms. Chang stated that she and DEC are concerned about the potential risks associated with this acquisition. As a result, she would like you to draft the representations and warranties to shift as much risk as possible, yet within reason, to TSI. In other words, she wants TSI to bear the bulk of the risk in regard to the representations and warranties.

Part 2: Additional Facts for the Assignment

Ms. Chang indicated that the following additional information has been provided by TSI or learned through the due diligence investigation of TSI and should be taken into account when drafting the representations and warranties and the necessary disclosure schedules:

Authority and No Conflict: TSI will obtain the necessary approvals of the shareholders of common stock and of the board of directors through unanimous written consent actions. Nothing was discovered in the due diligence process that indicates there would be any conflict for TSI to enter into this transaction.

Authorized Capital: No shares of TSI common or preferred stock have been issued other than as set forth in the basic fact scenario (see Chapter 2). Only the shareholders of common stock are entitled to vote on corporate matters. TSI has no obligation to issue additional shares to any other party and it does not have a stock option plan. All the issuances of shares of TSI were done properly, legally, and in accordance with TSI's corporate governance documents.

It was discovered in the due diligence process that Erin Mooney used her 10,000 shares of TSI preferred stock as collateral for a personal loan in the amount of $45,000. This loan is still outstanding with a current principle balance of $38,000. The bank was granted a security interest in Mooney's 10,000 shares of TSI preferred stock and still maintains that security interest.

Compliance with Legal Requirements and Governmental Authorizations: It appears that TSI is currently in compliance with any required legal requirements and governmental authorizations pertaining to its business and nothing in the due diligence investigation revealed any information to the contrary. TSI holds all the necessary licenses and permits to operate its business in the jurisdictions where it is required to do so.

Approximately six months ago, TSI received a notice from a local county government in Colorado that it was not complying with specific licensing requirements in regard to its employees who operate the "cherry pickers" utilized to remove high branches. TSI states it has since secured the proper licenses and remains in compliance.

In addition, during the past 12 months, the same county government notified TSI that on at least two occasions TSI did not secure the proper permits to trim or remove trees from public right of way areas.

CHAPTER 10

PRE-CLOSING COVENANTS

■ ■ ■

Brief Introduction to Pre-Closing Covenants

Covenants are promises by one party to the other party that create a duty to perform the promise. In a merger and acquisition, pre-closing covenants are utilized to delineate the responsibilities of the parties from the date of the execution of the agreement until the closing date. One of the main purposes of pre-closing covenants is to ensure that the closing conditions are satisfied and that the selling entity continues to operate in its normal course of business. The selling entity makes a more extensive set of covenants and thus bears the bulk of the obligation between the dates of execution and closing.

Pre-closing covenants can be affirmative—requiring the party to undertake or continue specific actions. These covenants can also be negative—requiring the party to refrain from taking specific actions without the consent of the other party or at all. In addition, there might be pre-closing covenants that require one party to notify the other party of certain events—such as receipt of a notice about a threatened lawsuit or an inquiry or offer of interest from another party.

Part 1: Pre-Closing Covenants Drafting Assignment

Melina Chang, the senior associate at McClelland, Springer & Henderson, LLC, DEC's outside counsel, has asked you to draft a number of pre-closing covenants that DEC is requiring of TSI. In particular, you are to draft the following TSI pre-closing covenants: Operation of TSI's Business; No Solicitation; Access to Information; Notification; Resignation of Officers and Directors; and Public Announcements.

Ms. Chang has indicated that you should draft the covenants in such a way as to provide DEC with adequate protection during the time frame between the execution of the merger and acquisition agreement and the closing, but to also be reasonable.

Part 2: Additional Facts for the Assignment

Ms. Chang indicated that the following additional information should be taken into account when drafting the pre-closing covenants:

<u>Operation of TSI's Business</u>: DEC requires that TSI continue to conduct and maintain its business and operations in the ordinary

course in an effort to preserve the business, all of the existing assets, and all of the relationships. Any changes outside the ordinary course require DEC's prior written consent, which DEC cannot unreasonably withhold or delay. Additionally, any material changes in the operation of the business (e.g. entering into a new material contract or licensing the trademark) require DEC's prior written consent, which DEC may withhold for any reason.

No Solicitation: DEC requires a strong no solicitation provision from TSI that covers TSI, its officers, directors, and any related or affiliated parties. This provision should be as encompassing as it can be. Under this provision, TSI must immediately notify DEC of any acquisition-related solicitation attempts made to any of the parties specifically referenced.

Access to Information: DEC requires prompt and on-going access to TSI's facilities; books, records, financial statements, and any other relevant documents; contracts; officers and directors; and any other data, material, or information requested. DEC has no desire to interrupt TSI's business operations in order for TSI to comply with this access to information covenant.

Notification: DEC requires that TSI promptly notify DEC of any material matter, event, condition, fact, or circumstance that may affect TSI's operations or its ability to consummate the transaction.

Resignation of Officers and Directors: As a part of this acquisition, DEC requires that all the current officers and directors of TSI resign from TSI effective as of the closing date. DEC requires these resignations be prepared and submitted prior to or at the closing of the transaction.

Public Announcements: DEC requires that its executive officers control all public announcements concerning this acquisition.

Part 3: Useful Resources for Students

Timothy R. Donovan and Jodi A. Simala, *Chapter 41. Mergers & Acquisition—The Definitive M&A Agreement—Covenants*, 2 Successful Partnering Between Inside and Outside Counsel § 41:28 (last updated Apr. 2014).

Brian Stuart Duba, *Chapter 17. Anatomy of An Acquisition Agreement—Covenants*, 33 Energy & Min. L. Found. § 17.08 (2012).

Alex Lee, *M&A Terms: Covenants Remain Consistent in Policing Target Operations*, Westlaw Mergers & Acquisitions Daily Briefing, 2014 WL 43934 (Dec. 2011).

CHAPTER 11

POST-CLOSING COVENANTS

■ ■ ■

Brief Introduction to Post-Closing Covenants

As discussed in Chapter 10, covenants are promises by one party to the other party that create a duty to perform the promise. Similar to pre-closing covenants, post-closing covenants are utilized in an acquisition to delineate the responsibilities of the parties after the closing date. These responsibilities are typically for a certain period of time post-closing. Post-closing covenants attempt to control the parties' behavior after the transaction has closed to protect the value of the selling company. As is the case in many merger and acquisition agreements, the seller is the party that makes the more extensive set of post-closing covenants and bears the majority of the responsibilities and obligations.

Part 1: Post-Closing Covenants Drafting Assignment

Melina Chang, the senior associate at McClelland, Springer & Henderson, LLC in charge of DEC's acquisition, has asked you to draft a number of the post-closing covenants of both TSI and DEC.

She has asked you to draft the following three TSI post-closing covenants: Confidentiality of Information; Non-Competition by TSI and the TSI common stockholders with DEC for two years post closing; and Non-Solicitation of DEC's employees (whether current DEC or former TSI employees) for one year post closing.

You have also been tasked with drafting the following two DEC post-closing covenants: DEC shall not reduce the compensation of any retained TSI employee during the initial twelve months after closing, and DEC shall offer an equivalent benefit package to any retained TSI employee for the initial twelve months after closing.

Ms. Chang has indicated that you should draft the post-closing covenants in such a way as to provide DEC with tight protection in regard to confidentiality, non-competition, and non-solicitation. In addition, she has indicated that you are to provide DEC with as much flexibility as possible in regard to its obligations to not reduce the pay or benefits of former TSI employees.

Part 2: Additional Facts for the Assignment

Ms. Chang has indicated that the following additional information should be taken into account when drafting the post-closing covenants of TSI:

Confidentiality of Information: This provision should cover TSI and the TSI common stockholders. Standard exceptions should be set forth. Additionally, a provision that provides DEC with notice of any exception that requires disclosure should be included.

Non-Competition: DEC would like this provision to be as broad in scope as is possible and to cover TSI and the TSI common stockholders. As a part of this post-closing covenant, you should draft a definition for both "territory" and "restricted business" and include those definitions at the end of the provision. DEC also wants to prevent TSI or the TSI common stockholders from interfering with any supplier or customer relationships (whether current or former in nature).

DEC is comfortable with the standard exception that allows for minimal ownership of a public company's stock, which operates in the "restricted business."

Non-Solicitation: DEC wants to prevent TSI and the TSI common stockholders from soliciting any DEC employee (whether or not a former TSI employee) for a period of at least twelve months after closing of the transaction. If the DEC employee was terminated (with or without cause) then the non-solicitation period is reduced to four months after closing.

The following information should be taken into account when drafting the post-closing covenants of DEC:

Compensation: DEC wants to be able to select which TSI employees it would like to retain, if it chooses to retain any. DEC is willing to pay any retained TSI employee compensation that is equivalent to the annual salary that the employee earned at TSI as of the closing date. However, DEC requires the flexibility to determine the manner in which the compensation will be paid (i.e. through a combination of an annual salary, DEC stock options, bonuses, etc.). DEC also wants the right to determine whether the newly hired employees are salaried or hourly.

Benefits: In regard to benefits, DEC is willing to offer a benefits package that is similar in scope and coverage, but not necessarily identical, to the package the retained employees had at TSI as of the closing date.

Part 3: Useful Resources for Students

Alan S. Gutterman, Part X. Acquisitions and Divestitures. *Chapter 291. Buying and Selling Businesses—Covenants and Agreements*, 26 Business Transactions Solutions § 291:139 (last updated Jun. 2014).

Alan S. Gutterman, *Part X. Acquisitions and Divestitures. Chapter 299. Sale of Partnerships and Limited Liability Companies— Covenants*, 29 Business Transactions Solutions § 299:20 (last updated Jun. 2014).

David M. Klein, *Chapter 5. Provisions of M&A Transaction Documents—Other Transaction Agreement Provisions—Post Closing Covenants*, IP in Mergers & Acquisitions § 5:32 (last updated Dec. 2013).

Alex Lee, *M&A Terms: Covenants Remain Consistent in Policing Target Operations*, Westlaw Mergers & Acquisitions Daily Briefing, 2014 WL 43934 (Dec. 2011).

CHAPTER 12

CLOSING CONDITIONS

■ ■ ■

Brief Introduction to Closing Conditions

According to the Restatement (Second) of Contracts §224, a condition is an uncertain event that must occur or be excused before performance under the contract becomes due. In the merger and acquisition agreement context, closing conditions must be satisfied before the closing of the transaction is required to occur. If the party who is obligated to fulfill the closing condition does not do so, the other party can walk away from the transaction and not proceed to closing, if it desires. While both the buyer and seller will make closing conditions, it is generally the seller that carries the greater burden. If the execution of the merger and acquisition agreement and closing are set to occur simultaneously, no closing conditions are required.

Both parties may stipulate to closing conditions that create a burden and require the party to secure something, such as shareholder approval, governmental approvals, or relevant consents and authorizations. The seller will typically agree to additional closing conditions such as (i) there has been no material adverse change in its business and operations; (ii) that the transaction is not illegal; and (iii) other status conditions. Lastly, the seller will stipulate that some or all of the representations and warranties are still true and correct as of the closing date, which condition is often referred to as the "bring-down" clause (as discussed in Chapter 28).

Closing conditions are crucial for transactions when there is a delay between the date the merger and acquisition agreement is executed and the date the closing takes place. Closing conditions exist to protect the parties in the transaction and to set the stage for a party to walk away from closing if the conditions go unmet.

Part 1: Closing Conditions Drafting Assignment

Melina Chang, the senior associate at McClelland, Springer & Henderson, LLC, DEC's outside counsel, has asked you to draft a number of the closing conditions for both parties. You are to draft the following mutual closing conditions so that each condition pertains to both DEC and TSI: Hart-Scott-Rodino Filing; No Governmental Orders; All Governmental Authority Consents and Approvals

Obtained; and Shareholder Approvals. In addition, you are to draft the following two closing conditions for TSI: Third Party Consents and No Material Adverse Effect.

Ms. Chang stated that she and DEC are concerned about TSI fulfilling all of its obligations and wants to be certain that DEC can avoid closing if it needs to do so. As a result, she would like you to draft the No Material Adverse Effect condition to benefit DEC to the greatest extent possible while remaining reasonable for TSI. In other words, she wants DEC to be fully protected.

Part 2: Additional Facts for the Assignment

Ms. Chang has indicated that the following additional information should be taken into account when drafting the closing conditions:

Mutual Conditions:

Nothing was discovered during the due diligence investigation or disclosed by the parties as relevant to, affecting, or requiring additional disclosure regarding the four mutual conditions set forth in Part 1. As a result, these four closing conditions should be drafted in a standard manner.

Conditions of TSI:

No Material Adverse Effect: In conjunction with this closing condition, you should include a definition for the term "material adverse effect" that benefits and protects DEC.

Third Party Consents: There are a number of third party consents required for this transaction. DEC would like TSI to use its best efforts to secure all the necessary consents prior to closing. In conjunction with this closing condition, you should include a definition for the term "best efforts."

In particular, DEC requires TSI to secure the following third party consents before DEC is obligated to close:

- Consent of landlord, Giant Real Estate Company, for the assignment of the TSI commercial lease to DEC.
- Consent of TSI's commercial lender, Big Bank, that TSI can enter into this acquisition.
- Any other consent that would have a material adverse effect on TSI or its business operations if not obtained prior to closing.

Part 3: Useful Resources for Students

Chapter 9. The Scope of Contractual Obligations, Topic 5. Conditions and Similar Events, Restatement (Second) of Contracts §§ 224–30 (1981).

Joseph B. Alexander, *The Material Adverse Change Clause (With Sample Language)*, 51 No. 5 Prac. Law. 11 (Oct. 2005).

Michael J. Chepiga & Paul C. Curnin, *Chapter 80. Mergers & Acquisitions, Part III. Characteristic Problems—Material Adverse Change*, 4B N.Y.Prac., Com. Litig. in New York State Courts § 80:20 (3d ed.) (last updated Sep. 2013).

Alan S. Gutterman, *Part V. Negotiated Acquisitions, Chapter 24. Merger Agreements—Purchaser's Closing Conditions*, 2 Corp. Couns. Gd. to Strategic Alliances § 24:47 (last updated Jun. 2014).

Chapter 2. Taxable Acquisitions in One Step: The Nontax Factors, Part II. Liability Considerations—Warranties, Representations, Covenants, and Conditions—Covenants and Conditions, Corporate Acquisitions § 2:28 (last updated Apr. 2014).

CHAPTER 13

TERMINATION

■ ■ ■

Brief Introduction to the Termination Provision

Under the general principles of contract law, the vast majority of contracts are subject to a right of termination, which means that a contract may be terminated in the event of a breach by the other party or upon the occurrence of specified termination rights in the contract. A merger and acquisition agreement typically contains a stand-alone termination provision that specifically addresses when, how, and by which party the agreement may be terminated. This provision may also specify post-termination rights and obligations of the parties.

The stand-alone termination provision should state the circumstances or events that give rise to the termination rights and indicate how the party seeking to terminate must proceed in order to exercise those termination rights. The termination provision may provide for either mutual termination by the parties or for unilateral termination by one party. In order to fully understand the rights under the termination provision, it should be read in conjunction with other sections of the merger and acquisition agreement that may give rise to or impact a party's right to terminate, such as the representations and warranties, covenants, closing conditions, and indemnification provisions.

Part 1: Termination Drafting Assignment

Even though DEC's counsel has assumed the role of drafting the initial version of the merger and acquisition agreement, for purposes of this assignment TSI's counsel has assumed responsibility as the lead drafter of the termination provision.

Lisa Goodman, the senior attorney at Williams & Bowers, PC who is managing the transaction for TSI, has tasked you with drafting the termination provision of the agreement. She has indicated to you that both parties are overly concerned about the other party's ability to terminate the deal. As a result, TSI desires to make this provision as mutual as possible and more in its favor where feasible. Ms. Goodman has also indicated that this provision will be a stand-alone section of the merger and acquisition agreement and should include standard termination rights for both parties, address the notice requirements for termination, and address the concerns resulting from the additional information about TSI and DEC provided below.

Part 2: Additional Facts for the Assignment

Ms. Goodman indicated that the following additional information should be taken into account when drafting the termination provision:

- While TSI desires to be acquired by DEC, TSI does not want to be in abeyance for an indefinite period of time and requires the ability to terminate the merger and acquisition agreement if closing has not occurred on or before 45 days after execution of the agreement, provided that the delay in closing is not caused by TSI or mutually agreed upon by TSI and DEC.

- DEC has indicated that it needs to seek financing from its commercial bank and lender in order to complete this acquisition. While it has sufficient cash on hand, DEC would prefer to finance the acquisition through a loan. DEC has already initiated the loan approval process, but it is unclear when the process will be complete.

- DEC is still completing its due diligence investigation of TSI and is concerned that additional issues may surface or arise as a result of the continuing investigation. As a result of the due diligence investigation, DEC has already discovered that TSI is facing a new lawsuit that raises concerns for DEC. This lawsuit centers around a complaint by one of TSI's largest commercial customers who claims that TSI removed and damaged a large number of trees at various golf courses owned by the customer. This customer, Big Golf Course Owner, has just recently filed a lawsuit seeking significant damages plus attorney's fees. The TSI Executives indicated that they are going to attempt to settle with Big Golf Course and that the parties have commenced settlement discussions. DEC would prefer this matter to be resolved within the next 45 days or it would like the ability to terminate the merger and acquisition agreement.

- Both parties must seek approval of the shareholders to move forward with the acquisition. If such approval is not achieved by the required percentage, the party not achieving approval wants the right to immediately terminate the merger and acquisition agreement with no further obligations.

- Rumors have surfaced that another company, which is a direct competitor of DEC, has an interest in acquiring

TSI if this current deal does not come to fruition. DEC is concerned about these rumors and would like the right to terminate the merger and acquisition agreement immediately if it learns that TSI is having discussions with any other party regarding a potential acquisition of TSI while TSI is in negotiations with DEC.

- Both parties have incurred significant expenses as a result of this potential acquisition. Neither party wants to be held responsible for the other party's out of pocket expenses if the acquisition is not completed. However, TSI desires the ability to recoup at least 50% of its expenses if TSI terminates the transaction due to DEC's failure to secure the necessary financing or if the closing has not occurred pursuant to the details in the first bullet point above.

Part 3: Useful Resources for Students

Afra Afsharipour, *Transforming the Allocation of Deal Risk Through Reverse Termination Fees*, 63 Vand. L. Rev. 1161 (Oct. 2010).

E. Thom Rumberger, Jr., Larry S. Adkison, & Elizabeth R. Cobey, *Chapter 9. An Overview of the Merger Agreement—Termination of the Agreement*, The Acquisition and Sale of Emerging Growth Companies: The M&A Exit § 9:39 (2d ed.) (last updated May 2009).

CHAPTER 14

INDEMNIFICATION

■ ■ ■

Brief Introduction to Indemnification

The indemnification section of a merger and acquisition agreement outlines the rights and obligations of the parties with respect to breaches of representations, warranties, covenants, or other provisions of the agreement. This section sets forth a party's rights for a breach that is discovered after the closing of the transaction has taken place. The main objective of indemnification is to cover the losses and expenses incurred by the buyer due to a material misrepresentation or a breach of the agreement by the seller.

Like many provisions in the merger and acquisition agreement, the indemnification section attempts to allocate the risk of the parties for post-closing breaches and liabilities. The buyer will want a broad indemnification provision that covers all potential liabilities that could arise for as long as possible, while the seller will want a narrow provision that significantly limits potential liability. Some of the crucial items addressed in the indemnification section of the merger and acquisition agreement are the length of the indemnification period, what types of losses are covered, the minimum and maximum dollar amount of the losses covered, whether funds will be escrowed to cover losses, and whether indemnification is the exclusive remedy.

Part 1: Indemnification Drafting Assignment

Melina Chang, the senior associate at McClelland, Springer & Henderson, LLC, DEC's outside counsel, has asked you to draft the indemnification section of the merger and acquisition agreement that pertains to TSI's obligation to indemnify DEC. Ms. Chang would like the provision to be drafted in such a way as to give DEC the broadest coverage possible for as long as is reasonably possible.

Part 2: Additional Facts for the Assignment

Ms. Chang has provided you with the following additional information to assist you in preparing the indemnification provision:

DEC wants to be fully indemnified by TSI for the following:

- Any inaccuracy or breach of a representation or warranty by TSI.

- Any breach or non completion of a covenant by TSI.
- Any breach of any other TSI obligation under the merger and acquisition agreement.

In addition to the information above, Ms. Chang has indicated the following matters should also be addressed:

- A notice provision addressing either party's obligation to provide the other party written notice of any assertion or action that falls within the indemnification provision.
- A provision that gives DEC the right to manage the negotiation, settlement, or litigation process regarding all assertions or claims that fall within the indemnification provision.
- A provision that provides TSI a reasonable right to approve any potential settlement or finalization of an assertion or action that falls within the indemnification provision.
- A provision that addresses the payment by TSI to DEC for the amount of any indemnified loss.
- Other standard indemnification section provisions (e.g. survival of representations, warranties and covenants; tax treatment of indemnification; effect of investigation).

DEC desires the following indemnification amounts and limitations:

- TSI's obligations to indemnify DEC commence after claims, in the aggregate, exceed $25,000. Once that dollar threshold is reached, TSI is responsible for additional losses.
- TSI's maximum amount of liability for all claims, in the aggregate, is $1,000,000. Once all aggregated claims exceed that dollar amount, TSI is no longer required to indemnify DEC.
- TSI must cover all of DEC's reasonable attorney's fees and expenses for any claims that fall within the indemnification provision.
- DEC does not want indemnification to be its sole or exclusive remedy under the merger and acquisition agreement.

Part 3: Useful Resources for Students

Hilary Bradbury, *Beyond Boilerplate: Drafting and Understanding Indemnification Clauses*, 51–JAN Advocate (Idaho) 13 (Jan. 2008).

William F. Griffin, Jr., *Chapter 12. Business Acquisition Agreements*, DEMC MA-CLE 12–1 (2013).

CHAPTER 15

MISCELLANEOUS PROVISIONS

■ ■ ■

Brief Introduction to Miscellaneous Provisions

Like most contracts, a merger and acquisition agreement contains a section of miscellaneous or general provisions that do not readily fit into another specific section. While these provisions are often viewed as boilerplate, they should be carefully reviewed to ensure that they do not negatively impact or affect the client and to ensure that the provisions are consistent with the other sections of the agreement.

The provisions contained in this section of the agreement generally deal with routine items such as (i) notice requirements, (ii) responsibility for expenses, (iii) significance of headings and captions, (iv) entire agreement and integration, (v) severability, (vi) amendment and modification, (vii) counterparts, (viii) successors and assigns, (ix) governing law, (x) selection of jurisdiction and venue, (xi) waiver of jury trial, (xii) arbitration, (xiii) no third-party beneficiary rights, and (xiv) force majeure. Because these provisions can have a significant impact on a party, they should not simply be dropped into the agreement. Rather, they must be carefully reviewed and considered in light of the entire transaction structure and agreement.

Part 1: Miscellaneous Provisions Drafting Assignment

TSI's counsel is taking the lead in drafting the miscellaneous provisions section of the merger and acquisition agreement.

Lisa Goodman, the senior attorney at Williams & Bowers, PC that is managing the transaction for TSI, has tasked you with drafting the miscellaneous provisions section of the agreement. Ms. Goodman indicated that she would like you to draft the provisions to be as favorable to TSI as reasonably possible. She wants you to prepare an initial draft of all the standard items typically found in this section of the merger and acquisition agreement. The items listed above should not be seen as an exhaustive list of miscellaneous provisions.

Part 2: Additional Facts for the Assignment

Ms. Goodman indicated that the following additional information should be taken into account when drafting the various miscellaneous provisions:

- Each party will be responsible for its own expenses associated with the merger and acquisition, including legal fees. However, TSI wants DEC to bear the burden of the Hart-Scott-Rodino filing fees and any and all other expenses related to such filing requirement.

- All notices and approvals must be in writing and can be delivered by hand (personal delivery), email, overnight delivery via a nationally recognized private carrier, or certified U.S. mail. However, if the notice is sent by certified mail it must be sent return receipt requested. Notices are required to be sent promptly.

- TSI wants to be certain that the "entire agreement" provision does not negate the requirements under the previously executed confidentiality agreement or any other agreements that pertain to the closing of the transaction.

- TSI indicated that an assignment of the agreement can only be effective if all the parties consent to it in writing. Additionally, any amendment or modification to the agreement requires the prior written consent of all parties.

- In the event of a dispute or litigation, TSI does not want to travel outside of its home state. TSI requires that any matters subject to dispute must be resolved in its home state with its state's law as the governing law. Additionally, TSI prefers disputes to be settled via arbitration.

- TSI wants to be able to compel specific performance under the agreement in addition to any other remedies that are available.

Part 3: Useful Resources for Students

Matthew K. Hobbs, *Boilerplate Provisions: Traps Exposed for the Drafter*, 31—JUL Colo. Law. 105 (July 2002).

Jeremiah T. Reynolds, *Defending Boilerplate in Contracts*, 31—DEC L.A. Law. 10 (December 2008).

Gisela M. Munoz, *Writing Tips for the Transactional Attorney*, 21 No. 3 Prac. Real Est. Law. 33 (May 2005).

Liz Klingensmith & Larry Huelbig, *A Watched Pot Never Boils: Preventing Boilerplate Provisions from Bubbling Over*, 48—OCT Hous. Law. 18 (September/October 2010).

CHAPTER 16

PREPARING A MARK-UP DRAFT AND COMMENTS

■ ■ ■

Brief Introduction to Mark-ups and Comments

An important skill set for every transactional lawyer is the ability to review a draft of a document and respond to that document with comments and concerns or with a mark-up (red-lined version) of the document. The comment and mark-up process are a part of the overall negotiation process.

In order to provide comments or prepare a mark-up, the lawyer must clearly understand the client's goals and objectives. This will enable the lawyer to best address the client's objectives in the comments or mark-up and to suggest revisions that place his client in a better position. The lawyer and client must work together to determine how aggressive to be and how far to push with the comments or mark-ups without jeopardizing the transaction.

Part 1: Mark-up and Feedback Drafting Assignment

You are a junior attorney at Williams & Bowers, PC, TSI's outside counsel. Lisa Goodman, the senior attorney at Williams & Bowers, PC that is managing the transaction for TSI, has tasked you with reviewing the representations and warranties section of the merger and acquisition agreement and preparing a mark-up of that section for her and TSI's benefit.

The mark-up should reflect all proposed changes, including additions, deletions, comments, and any follow-up questions for TSI. Ms. Goodman has reminded you that this section was drafted by DEC's counsel and is likely to benefit DEC more than TSI. She has advised you to take that into consideration when you are reviewing the section and preparing your mark-up.

(Students can use the representations and warranties each drafted for the Chapter 8 assignment to create the mark-up or students could exchange representations and warranties from the Chapter 8 assignment to create the mark-up of a classmate's assignment).

Part 2: Additional Facts for the Assignment

Ms. Goodman has indicated that the following additional information should be taken into account when preparing the markup of the representations and warranties section:

- Erin Mooney, a TSI outside director and common stockholder, is not in a position to pay off the $45,000 personal loan ($38,000 outstanding balance) that is collateralized by her TSI preferred stock until she receives her portion of the money due her from DEC's acquisition of TSI. As a result, she will not be able to pay off the loan and ask the bank to release its security interest until after closing takes place. Erin notified TSI that she did not make her most recent payment on the loan. In order to prevent potential issues, TSI made the payment on Erin's behalf, but it was made ten business days late.

- TSI is in the process of renewing many of its county licenses and is doing so in a timely manner. As far as TSI is aware, all of its licenses are current and it is not operating in any county without the requisite license.

- For the third time this year, TSI received notice of a failure to secure a permit and was fined $2,000. This notice was issued from a different county than the prior two notices that DEC discovered in its due diligence investigation. TSI is in the process of implementing a new system to better manage the permitting process to ensure that TSI secures all necessary permits prior to undertaking a job.

- TSI is only willing to share limited information regarding its legal proceedings because it does not want to jeopardize its attorney-client privilege. TSI is willing to share publicly available information about the ABC Management Company and Big Golf Course Owner lawsuits (i.e. anything that has been filed with the courts) and information about the workers' compensation claim filed by Sally Dawson. TSI is not willing to share any specific details regarding the threatened lawsuit by Ms. Dawson for emotional distress. TSI was recently notified of another potential lawsuit resulting from a car accident involving one its employees who was driving a TSI-owned truck. TSI and its vehicle insurance company are working together to resolve this matter as the employee claims he was not at fault. The accident is still under investigation. TSI does not have an estimate of the potential cost of this accident. Additionally, the truck was damaged and requires significant repairs to be usable.

- TSI's counsel received a letter this week from Thorny Shrubs regarding its infringement of the TSI trademark. Thorny Shrubs, Inc. has indicated it wants to set up a call between each company's lawyers to discuss and resolve the matter. Thorny Shrubs, Inc. indicated that it does not believe it is infringing the TSI Trademark, but TSI and its counsel believe it is simply a stalling tactic. Based on consultation with its intellectual property counsel, TSI believes that Thorny Shrubs is clearly infringing and that once the lawyers speak the matter will be resolved. However, final resolution of this matter is unlikely to happen until after closing of the acquisition takes place.

- In the ordinary course of business, TSI increased the amount outstanding under its line of credit with Big Bank from $225,000 to $246,000. This was as a result of a purchase of a new truck to replace an old one that was at the end of its useful life. TSI remains current in all payments due under the line of credit. The line of credit agreement contains a change in control provision that indicates that upon a change of control in TSI, the entire amount becomes immediately due and payable. However, Big Bank has indicated that it is willing to assign the line of credit to DEC upon receipt of certain financial statements from DEC and a clean credit check.

- TSI reached a settlement with its website developer, Webmasters Limited, regarding the alleged breach of contract claim and failure to pay. The parties reached an agreement as to a reduced payment from TSI to satisfy the contract terms in full. TSI intends to pay the negotiated settlement amount within two business days.

- TSI offers its top 30 customers various incentives under its form services agreement. These customers receive a 5% discount on any fee for a service they receive. They also receive an additional 5% discount if they pay their bill within 15 calendar days of the invoice date. In most instances these customers take advantage of the 5% discount for early payment. Lastly, these 30 customers receive a cash bonus payment of $100 for every customer they refer to TSI who enters into a services agreement for services totaling $3,000 or more over a twelve month period.

Part 3: Useful Resources for Students

William B. Payne, *Responding to the Buyer's First Draft of the M&A Agreement: Don't Do Anything Until You Call The Client!*, 52 No. 2 Prac. Law. 19 (Apr. 2006).

David M. Klein, *Chapter 5. Provisions of M&A Transaction Documents—The Process*, IP in Mergers & Acquisitions § 5:5 (last updated Dec. 2013).

Vincent A. Wellman, *What's Special About Contract Drafting?: Theme Introduction*, 92 Mich. B.J. 25 (June 2013).

CHAPTER 17

DIRECTOR AND SHAREHOLDER RESOLUTIONS

■ ■ ■

Brief Introduction to Board of Directors and Shareholder Resolutions

Merger and acquisition transactions may require approval of both the board of directors or other governing body and the shareholders or owners. While the approvals required will depend on the entity and its corporate governance documents, as well as general corporate law, in almost every acquisition some approval of either the board of directors, the shareholders, or both will be necessary.

In many cases, corporate entities seek such approvals through a written consent process that involves the preparation and execution of a board of directors' or shareholders' written consent action. The written consent process is also controlled by the entity's corporate governance documents and general corporate law, which will dictate the consent percentage required—a majority, super majority, or unanimous—to effectuate the written consent. The written consents should set forth all matters the board of directors or shareholders are consenting to in regard to the acquisition.

Part 1: Resolutions Drafting Assignment

Melina Chang, the senior associate at McClelland, Springer & Henderson, LLC, DEC's outside counsel, has asked you to prepare the written consent action for the DEC board of directors to approve the transaction with TSI. She has indicated that you should use all of the information you have learned to date regarding the transaction to prepare the written consent and that such consent action should include all standard resolutions.

Ms. Chang has indicated that the corporate governance documents for DEC require unanimous written consent for board of directors written consent actions.

Part 2: Additional Facts for the Assignment

Ms. Chang has provided you with the following additional information to assist you in your preparation of the DEC board of directors written consent:

- DEC has created a wholly owned subsidiary, TSI NEWCO, Inc. (TSINI), which is a Nevada corporation. DEC will merge TSI with and into TSINI upon closing of the transaction and TSINI will be the surviving corporation. Immediately after closing, TSINI will be renamed Tree Services, Inc., a Nevada corporation, and will remain a wholly owned subsidiary of DEC.

- All shareholders owning common stock of TSI will sell their shares to DEC in exchange for the agreed upon consideration. DEC will pay the TSI preferred stock shareholders their liquidation preference and guaranteed dividend at closing.

- The DEC board of directors is thrilled with, and fully supportive of, the acquisition and the structure that has been proposed.

- The DEC board of directors has agreed to make employment offers to Melissa Green and Thomas Shrub, but not Susan Brown. The board fully supports these employment offers and believes the employment offers will greatly benefit DEC and make for a smooth transition.

- The base terms of the employment offers to Ms. Green and Mr. Shrub are as follows:

  o The board approves the employment of Melissa Green as Senior Vice President, with a base salary of $400,000 and a potential annual bonus of up to 20% of her base salary.

  o The board approves the employment of Thomas Shrub as Vice President, with a base salary of $325,000 and the issuance of 5,000 DEC common stock options.

- The DEC board of directors has agreed to nominate Melissa Green as a new board member and to make that nomination at the next annual meeting of shareholders. The board fully supports this nomination and believes that Melissa Green will bring value to the DEC board of directors.

- In the event Melissa Green secures the necessary shareholder vote to serve as a member of the DEC board of directors, DEC will be required to amend its corporate governance documents to allow for up to ten directors (the documents currently provide for a maximum of nine directors).

- The DEC corporate governance documents require that shareholders approve any increase in the number of directors on the board.

- The DEC board of directors has empowered executive officers Fred Wilcox and Margaret Fife to expend any funds necessary to effectuate the merger and acquisition, and to execute and file any documents related to the transaction.

- The DEC board of directors reviewed the most recent version of the merger and acquisition agreement and found it acceptable. The board is comfortable if revisions must be made to the agreement in order to finalize it so long as such revisions do not impact any of the financial terms or require material changes. DEC's board of directors requires that any revisions to the merger and acquisition agreement be either recommended or approved by outside counsel.

Part 3: Useful Resources for Students

William M. McKenzie, *Chapter 8. Directors, Officers, and Agents, II. Meeting and Actions of Board—Consent to Action of Board of Directors*, 2 Cal. Transactions Forms—Bus. Entities § 8:57 (last updated Mar. 2014).

Alan S. Gutterman, *Part X. Acquisitions and Divestitures, Chapter 297. Corporate Mergers—Recommendation or Resolution of Directors*, 29 Business Transactions Solutions § 297:33 (last updated Jun. 2014).

Celia R. Taylor, *"A Delicate Interplay": Resolving the Contract and Corporate Law Tension in Mergers*, 74 Tul. L. Rev. 561, 574–580 (1999).

Chapter 74. Corporation, XV. Merger and Consolidation—Stockholder's Resolution—Adopting Plan and Agreement of Merger, 6B Am. Jur. Legal Forms 2d § 74:1651 (last updated May 2014).

Miriam P. Hechler, *The Role of the Corporate Attorney Within the Takeover Context: Loyalties to Whom?*, 21 Del. J. Corp. L. 943 (1996).

Clifford R. Ennico, *Part IV. Closely Held Corporations, Chapter 15. Meetings of Directors and Shareholders—The Nearly Forgotten Art of Drafting Corporate Resolutions*, Forms for Small Business Entities § 15:2 (2014).

CHAPTER 18

THIRD PARTY CONSENTS

■ ■ ■

Brief Introduction to Third Party Consents

In many acquisitions, the consent of third parties may be necessary to close the transaction. Third party consents may also be required before a contract can be assigned and assumed by the buyer. While the issue of third party consents is more prevalent in an asset purchase transaction, these consents are often required in mergers and acquisitions when there is a change in control of ownership.

The third parties that may have the right to consent to the transaction or to an assignment and assumption of a contract include lenders, landlords, customers, suppliers, and others. Generally, the closing conditions will include provisions that require the seller to request and secure the necessary third party consents to the transaction or the assignment of material contracts prior to the closing.

Part 1: Consent to Assignment of Lease Drafting Assignment

You are a junior associate at Williams & Bowers, PC, TSI's outside counsel. Lisa Goodman, the senior associate managing the TSI transaction, has requested that you draft a letter that TSI will send to its landlord, Giant Real Estate Company, seeking consent to the assignment of the commercial lease to DEC. The letter should include a form of consent for the landlord to sign to consent to the assignment of the lease from TSI to DEC. DEC is requiring that TSI secure this consent prior to the closing of the transaction and that the landlord consent is a condition of closing.

Part 2: Additional Facts for the Assignment

In order to prepare the letter to the landlord requesting consent to the assignment of the lease and the form of consent, Ms. Goodman provided you with the following additional information:

- You should refer to the commercial lease agreement between Giant Real Estate Company and Tree Services, Inc. (Lease Agreement) included in Appendix B in conjunction with the due diligence assignment (see Chapter 6) for the pertinent information regarding the landlord, landlord's consent rights, and proper notice requirements.

- You should assume that the Lease Agreement was effectively renewed for a second five-year term commencing on June 1, 2014.

- DEC is willing to assume the Lease Agreement "as is" without any changes to the current Lease Agreement's terms and conditions.

- DEC wants the assignment of the Lease Agreement from TSI to DEC to be effective as of the closing date of the acquisition.

- DEC is requiring that TSI secure the consent of the landlord to this Lease Agreement assignment before it is willing to close the transaction, which is scheduled to take place in one month, so time is of the essence.

Part 3: Useful Resources for Students

E. Thom Rumberger, Jr., Larry S. Adkison, & Elizabeth R. Cobe, *Chapter 5. Structuring the M&A Exit Transaction—Determining What Should be Bought and Sold: Some Assets, All the Assets, or the Entity—Key Considerations—Third Party Consents*, The Acquisition and Sale of Emerging Growth Companies: The M&A Exit § 5:6 (last updated May 2009).

Richard M. Frome, *Drafting Landlord Consent to Assignment and Subletting Clauses (With Sample Clauses)*, 18 No. 3 Prac. Real Est. Law. 7 (May 2002).

Alan S. Gutterman, *Part V. Negotiated Acquisitions, Chapter 21. Negotiated Acquisitions—Purchase and Sale Transactions—Closing Procedures and Documents—Third-Party Consents and Permits*, 2 Corp. Couns. Gd. to Strategic Alliances § 21:79 (last updated June 2014).

CHAPTER 19

ASSIGNMENTS AND ASSUMPTIONS

■ ■ ■

Brief Introduction to Assignments and Assumptions

In conjunction with the third party consents discussed in Chapter 18, many contracts must be assigned by the seller and assumed by the buyer as part of the overall transaction. The assignment and assumption agreement transfers the rights and obligations under a specific contract from the seller to the buyer and is generally effective on the closing date of the acquisition. In most cases, the buyer assumes all of the rights and obligations of the seller under the contract as of a specific date. However, in limited circumstances the buyer may limit the rights and obligations that it assumes with the seller responsible for the un-assumed obligations.

Part 1: Assignment and Assumption of Lease Agreement Drafting Assignment

You are a junior associate at Williams & Bowers, PC, TSI's outside counsel. Lisa Goodman, the senior associate managing the TSI transaction, has requested that you draft the "assignment and assumption agreement" for TSI's commercial lease. DEC will assume all the rights and obligations of TSI under the commercial lease effective as of the closing date of the transaction.

Part 2: Additional Facts for the Assignment

In order to help you prepare the assignment and assumption agreement for the commercial lease, Ms. Goodman has provided you with the following additional information:

- You should refer to the commercial lease agreement between Giant Real Estate Company and Tree Services, Inc. (Lease Agreement) provided in Appendix B as a part of the due diligence assignment (see Chapter 6) for the pertinent information regarding the Lease Agreement and all the relevant rights and obligations.
- You should assume that the Lease Agreement was effectively renewed for a second five-year term commencing on June 1, 2014.

- DEC is assuming the Lease Agreement "as is" without any changes to the current Lease Agreement terms, conditions, or obligations.

- The assignment and assumption agreement shall be governed by Colorado law and nothing in the assignment and assumption agreement shall supersede or override the terms of the merger and acquisition agreement.

- As a part of the assignment and assumption of the Lease Agreement, the landlord requires that DEC submit a security deposit in the amount of $4,500 to replace the original TSI security deposit of the same amount that Giant Real Estate Company will refund to TSI.

- TSI wants to include an indemnification provision in this agreement that makes it clear that DEC will indemnify TSI for any liabilities that arise regarding the Lease Agreement commencing on or occurring after the effective date of the assignment and assumption.

Part 3: Useful Resources for Students

Williston on Contracts, *Chapter 74. Assignment of Contracts*, 29 Williston on Contracts §§ 74:1–74:9 and §§ 74:34–74:40 (May 2014).

Irene Calboli, *Trademark Assignment "With Goodwill": A Concept Whose Time Has Gone*, 57 Fla. L. Rev. 771 (September 2005).

Randall D. McClanahan, *Assignment, Delegation, and Choice of Law Provisions in Commercial Agreements*, 57 No. 3 Prac. Law. 15 (June. 2011).

Glenda K. Harnard, *Landlord and Tenant, Part N. Assignments, Subleases, and Mortgages, Part A. Assignments*, 14 Maryland Law Enc. Landlord and Tenant §§ 37–40 (last updated Jun. 2014).

CHAPTER 20

PROVIDING FEEDBACK

■ ■ ■

Brief Introduction to Providing Feedback

An important skill for every lawyer regardless of the type of practice is the ability to provide constructive feedback to junior attorneys, paralegals, and administrative assistants who prepare initial drafts of letters or documents. It is often difficult to provide this type of feedback in a balanced manner so that the recipient construes it as constructive and instructional rather than as disparaging and negative.

The goal of feedback is two-fold. The first goal is for the initial drafter to be provided with enough information that he is able to revise the letter or document so that it meets the request. The second goal is to provide the initial drafter with sufficient feedback so that he can improve his drafting skills. Many people, including lawyers, are uncomfortable critiquing the work or writing styles of others, but as a lawyer progresses through his legal career, this is a skill that must be learned and developed.

Part 1: Providing Feedback Assignment

You are now a senior associate at Williams & Bowers, PC, TSI's outside counsel. You just received the initial draft of the letter requesting that the landlord consent to the assignment of TSI's commercial lease to DEC. The letter was prepared by a classmate pursuant to the Chapter 18 assignment. Your task is to provide constructive feedback to the junior associate (classmate) that prepared the letter. It is at your discretion how you provide feedback—handwritten or via electronic changes and comments.

Part 2: Additional Facts for the Assignment

The following additional information should be taken into account when providing feedback regarding the letter requesting consent to assignment of the lease:

- The lease was renewed for a second five-year term commencing on June 1, 2014.
- DEC is assuming the lease "as is" without any changes to the current lease's terms and conditions.

- The assignment of the lease from TSI to DEC is to be effective as of the closing date of the acquisition.
- The consent of the landlord must be secured before DEC is willing to close the transaction, which is scheduled to take place in one month.

Part 3: Useful Resources for Students

Edward M. O'Brien & Spencer J. Brooks, *Best Practice: Editing—Streamlining the Editing Process*, 30 T.M. Cooley L. Rev. 207 (2013).

Gerald Lebovits, <<*strikethrough*>> *PROVE* <<*end strikethrough*>> *PROOF IT WITH* <<*strikethrough*>> *REVISION* <<*end strikethrough*>> *RE-VISION-PART I*, 81–SEP N.Y. St. B.J. 64 (September 2009).

Gerald Lebovits, <<*strikethrough*>> *PROVE* <<*end strikethrough*>> *PROOF IT WITH* <<*strikethrough*>> *REVISION* <<*end strikethrough*>> *RE-VISION-PART II*, 81–OCT N.Y. St. B.J. 64 (October 2009).

Suzanne E. Rowe, *Perfect Proofing: 10 Steps Towards Error-Free Documents*, 67–DEC Or. St. B. Bull. 33 (Dec. 2006).

CHAPTER 21

CERTIFICATE OF MERGER

■ ■ ■

Brief Introduction to the Certificate of Merger

In conjunction with a merger of two corporate entities, both entities are required to file a Certificate of Merger, Articles of Merger, or a Statement of Merger with the Secretary of State's office in their respective state of incorporation. This document effectuates the legal merger of the two entities.

The merger is generally effective upon the filing of the document unless it specifically stipulates a different or later effective date. The filings with each state should be made simultaneously or should state the same effective date in order to avoid any potential issues from inconsistent timing. Each state has its own set of laws governing the disclosure required in the Certificate, Articles, or Statement of Merger.

Part 1: Certificate, Articles, or Statement of Merger Drafting Assignment

A.   You are a junior associate at McClelland, Springer & Henderson, LLC, DEC's outside counsel. Melina Chang, the senior associate managing the DEC transaction, has requested that you prepare the Articles of Merger for filing with the Nevada Secretary of State.

B.   You are a junior associate at Williams & Bowers, PC, TSI's outside counsel. Lisa Goodman, the senior associate managing the TSI transaction, has requested that you prepare the Statement of Merger for filing with the Colorado Secretary of State.

Part 2: Additional Facts for the Assignment

In order to prepare the Articles of Merger and Statement of Merger, the following additional information has been provided:

- Both DEC and TSI want their respective filings to be made at least three business days prior to the closing date of the transaction. The filings should indicate that the merger is to be effective as of the closing date, which is two weeks from today's date. The merger and acquisition agreement has been approved, if required, by the boards of directors and shareholders of all the entities involved in the transaction.

- DEC has formed a wholly owned subsidiary in Nevada, TSI NEWCO, Inc. (TSINI), to effectuate the merger. TSI will merge with and into TSINI and TSINI will be the surviving entity. The current officers of DEC are also the officers and directors of TSINI.

Pertinent information about each entity is as follows:

> Dutch Elm Company, Inc. (a Nevada C corporation)
> 10000 Patrick Lane
> Las Vegas, NV 89118
> Registered Agent: Fred Wilcox
>
> TSI NEWCO, Inc. (a Nevada C corporation)
> 10000 Patrick Lane
> Las Vegas, NV 89118
> Registered Agent: Fred Wilcox
>
> Tree Services, Inc. (a Colorado C corporation)
> 6789 120th Street
> Commerce City, CO 80022
> Registered Agent: Melissa Green

Part 3: Useful Resources for Students

Chapter 61. Combination, Consolidation and Merger of Corporations, III. Steps and Proceedings to Effect Consolidation and Merger, 15 Fletcher Cyc. Corp. §§ 7066–7074 (last updated Apr. 2014).

Alan S. Gutterman, *Part X. Acquisitions and Divestitures, Chapter 297. Corporate Mergers—Articles of Merger or Share Exchange*, 29 Business Transactions Solutions § 297:40 (last updated Jun. 2014).

CHAPTER 22

HART-SCOTT-RODINO FILING

■ ■ ■

Brief Introduction to Hart-Scott-Rodino Filing

In many mergers and acquisitions, the companies must comply with the Hart-Scott-Rodino Antitrust Improvements Act (HSR), which requires that the merger be approved by U.S. antitrust authorities before it can be finalized. A set of Federal Trade Commission guidelines set forth whether the merger and acquisition transaction meets the HSR criteria and if so, the companies must file an HSR form regarding the proposed merger and acquisition. There is a mandatory 30-day waiting period after the HSR form is filed. Once that waiting period has passed the acquisition can be completed and finalized, provided there is not a request for additional information or a full investigation.

Part 1: Hart-Scott-Rodino Filing Drafting Assignment

You are a junior associate at McClelland, Springer & Henderson, LLC, DEC's outside counsel. Jeffrey McClelland, the partner overseeing the HSR filing on behalf of DEC, has asked you to prepare a draft of the initial HSR form that DEC will file regarding the transaction. He has requested that you access the Notification and Report Form for Certain Mergers and Acquisitions (16 CFR Part 803) from the Federal Trade Commission's website at www.ftc.gov. Mr. McClelland has asked you to complete the form and print it for his review.

Part 2: Additional Facts for the Assignment

You should refer to the factual information provided to you in Chapter 2—Fact Scenario in preparation of the HSR form.

In addition, Mr. McClelland provided the following additional information to assist you in preparing the form:

- Margaret Fife, DEC's Chief Financial Officer, will execute the document on behalf of the company and is the primary DEC contact person. Bernard Thompson will act as a back-up contact person on behalf of DEC and TSINI.

- DEC formed a wholly owned subsidiary, TSI NEWCO, Inc. (TSINI) to effectuate the merger and TSINI is a Nevada C corporation.

- DEC, TSINI, and TSI's fiscal years all end on December 31.
- TSINI is the entity that will ultimately acquire 100% of the issued and outstanding common stock of TSI as part of the transaction and TSI will be merged with and into TSINI. TSINI will be the surviving entity, will remain a wholly owned subsidiary of DEC after the transaction, and will change its name to Tree Services Inc., a Nevada corporation.
- TSINI will assume all of the assets, liabilities, rights and obligations of TSI—no assets or liabilities have been carved out of the transaction except for the following:
  - TSI workers' compensation claims based on injuries that occurred prior to the closing date.
  - TSI's revolving line of credit and security agreement with Big Bank in the amount of $750,000 ($246,000 currently outstanding and unpaid).
- Neither DEC nor TSINI currently own any shares of the common stock or preferred stock of TSI or have any other economic interests in TSI.
- As of the date of the HSR filing, TSI's common stock is valued at $10.00 per share.
- Neither DEC nor TSI are publicly traded companies or SEC reporting companies.
- DEC uses an outside auditing firm to prepare audited financial statements for its own use.
- TSI uses an outside accounting firm to prepare unaudited financial statements for its own use.
- The NAICS Industry Code for both DEC and TSI is 561730—Landscaping Services and all of the revenues for each company are attributable to that specific code.
- DEC has not previously acquired any other business that operates in the same NAICS Industry Code or Segment.
- None of the officers, directors, or shareholders of DEC or TSI own an interest in any other company that operates in the same NAICS Industry Code or Segment.
- Mr. McClelland will provide the necessary copies of the merger documents, audit reports, analyses and reports (both internal and third party), confidential information memoranda, financial statements, and any other documents that must be attached to and filed with the HSR form.

Part 3: Useful Resources for Students

Antitrust Issues in Acquisitions and Divestitures, 214 Corporate Counsel's Primers 1 (Oct. 2011).

Alan S. Gutterman, *Part X. Acquisitions and Divestitures, Chapter 297. Corporate Mergers—Notification and Review Requirements*, 29 Business Transactions Solutions § 297:47 (last updated June 2014).

Barry J. Lipson, *Part IV. Business Transactions, Chapter 28. Antitrust Laws—Premerger Notification*, 2 Advising Small Businesses § 28:38 (last updated Apr. 2014.)

Joseph W. Bartlett, *Part III. Buyouts, Chapter 16. LBOs, MBOs, Recapitalizations, Mergers, and Asset Sales—Hart-Scott-Rodino*, Equity Fin. § 16.12 (2014).

CHAPTER 23

LEGAL OPINION OF SELLER'S COUNSEL

■ ■ ■

Brief Introduction to Legal Opinions

A legal opinion is a professional opinion generally issued in the form of a letter by an attorney to another party that expresses legal conclusions as to certain matters. Legal opinions can cover a wide range of topics and areas, but in the context of a merger and acquisition transaction the selling company's counsel may be required to provide a legal opinion regarding certain aspects of its client, the seller, as they pertain to the transaction. The purpose of the opinion is to provide the buyer with added protection or comfort in proceeding with the transaction. This type of opinion letter is a third-party opinion as it requires the seller's counsel to issue an opinion about its client, the seller, to the other side, the buyer. There are both positive and negative aspects to agreeing to issue and fulfill an opinion letter request.

Part 1: Legal Opinion of Seller's Counsel Drafting Assignment

You are a junior associate at Williams & Bowers, PC, TSI's outside counsel. Lisa Goodman, the senior associate managing the TSI transaction, has requested that you prepare the initial draft of the opinion letter that Williams & Bowers will issue to DEC regarding the transaction. Ms. Goodman has indicated that the request from DEC and its outside counsel is for a standard opinion letter that addresses the following:

- TSI validly exists and is in good standing.
- TSI has the ability to undertake the transaction and to enter into the merger and acquisition agreement and related documents.
- TSI has taken, or will have taken by closing, all the necessary corporate actions and formalities to effectuate the transaction (e.g. board of directors and shareholder approval).
- TSI will be legally bound by the merger and acquisition agreement and related documents.

Part 2: Additional Facts for the Assignment

Ms. Goodman provided the following additional information to assist you in your preparation of the legal opinion:

- The firm has copies of TSI's corporate governance documents that indicate it validly exists as of today's date and has done so since its incorporation in January 2003. All corporate filings are current and TSI has maintained accurate records and minutes of its shareholder and board of directors meetings.

- The firm has a copy of TSI's Certificate of Good Standing issued by the Colorado Secretary of State as of today's date.

- The firm prepared the TSI board of directors and shareholders unanimous written consent actions that approve all aspects of the transaction and stipulate that the merger and acquisition agreement and related documents are acceptable and approved with minor changes permitted. The unanimous consent actions of the board of directors and shareholders have been fully executed by all parties as of two days ago and the firm has a copy of the executed consent actions.

Part 3: Useful Resources for Students

Lilian Blackshear, *Wait . . . What Did I Just Say?: What Lawyers Need To Be Concerned About When Issuing Third-Party Closing Opinions*, 10 Transactions: Tenn. J. Bus. L. 71 (Fall 2008).

A. Sidney Holderness, Jr., Brooke Wunnicke, & Linda I. Dole, *Legal Opinion Letters Formbook—Chapters 3–13* (2011).

M. John Sterba, Jr. & Richard T. McDermott, *Chapter 2—Elements of an Opinion Letter*, Legal Opinion Letters §§ 2.1–2.16 (2013).

Chapter 24

Escrow Agreement

■ ■ ■

Brief Introduction to the Escrow Agreement

The escrow agreement sets out the specific terms and conditions regarding any funds to be placed in escrow as a part of closing the transaction. In many mergers and acquisitions, it is typical for a portion of the cash consideration to be held in an escrow account for a certain period of time to satisfy claims that may arise after the closing of the transaction for which the seller remains liable. An escrow account may also be utilized to set aside a portion of the consideration that is not a guaranteed payment to the seller, but one that can be earned through meeting some type of post-closing condition (e.g. an earn-out). The escrow agreement will be between the buyer, seller, and the escrow agent and will set forth how the escrowed funds are to be held and distributed by the escrow agent.

Part 1: Escrow Agreement Drafting Assignment

You are a junior associate at McClelland, Springer & Henderson, LLC, DEC's outside counsel. Melina Chang, the senior associate in charge of the transaction, has tasked you with drafting the escrow agreement pertaining to the funds that will be placed in escrow as part of the closing in order to satisfy any potential TSI pre-closing litigation claims that arise or are paid post-closing. Ms. Chang has stated that she wants you to prepare a buyer friendly escrow agreement with all of the standard terms and conditions, but noted that it should also be reasonable to TSI.

Alternative Assignment: Ms. Chang has requested that you draft the following escrow agreement provisions: (i) deposit of the funds; (ii) investment of the escrow funds; (iii) release of the escrow funds; and (iv) indemnification of the escrow agent.

Part 2: Additional Facts for the Assignment

You should refer to Chapter 8—Merger Consideration for the specific details regarding the amount to be escrowed and other relevant information pertaining to the escrowed funds.

Ms. Chang provided you with the following additional information in order to prepare the escrow agreement:

- The escrow agent agreed to by both parties is Nevada State Bank.

- DEC shall deposit the funds in the escrow account by wire transfer at closing. Such funds shall be immediately available to satisfy the claims as more fully described in the merger and acquisition agreement (see Chapter 8—Merger Consideration and Chapter 9—Representations and Warranties).

- DEC and TSI have mutually agreed that the funds shall be invested in an interest bearing account or in short-term certificates of deposits with maturity dates of 30 days or less. Such investments must be made in U.S. banks or trust companies. DEC and TSI may stipulate other investment instructions, but such instructions must be written and executed by both parties before the escrow agent is required to comply with them.

- Any interest or returns earned on the escrow funds become part of the escrow amount that DEC may make a claim against. TSI is entitled to receive any interest or returns on escrow funds remaining at the end of the escrow period.

- The escrow funds exist solely to satisfy the indemnification related claims and may be released periodically or all at once. In order for the escrow agent to release the funds, the following must occur:

  o DEC must submit a written notice of a claim with specific details to both TSI and the escrow agent.

  o TSI has five business days to object in writing to any DEC claim on the funds to both DEC and the escrow agent with reasonable detail of its reasons for the objection.

  o If the escrow agent does not receive an objection from TSI within the time limit, it shall release the funds by wire transfer to DEC.

  o If the escrow agent receives an objection within the required time frame, it will not release any of the claimed funds to DEC, but instead will wait until it receives either joint written instructions from DEC and TSI regarding the claim on the funds and how it should be handled, or it receives a final non-appealable order from any court regarding the claim on the funds.

- o If TSI only objects to a portion of the claim on the funds, the escrow agent can release those funds not subject to dispute to DEC by wire transfer.
- o The escrow agent shall release any remaining funds to TSI by wire transfer no later than 15 business days after the end of the escrow period. However, if an unresolved claim or dispute regarding funds exists, the escrow agent will not release the unresolved claim or disputed funds.
- Upon reasonable notice, both DEC and TSI can inspect the escrow agent's books and records regarding the escrow account.
- The escrow agent will provide monthly account statements to both DEC and TSI.
- DEC and TSI can mutually agree to replace the escrow agent.
- DEC and TSI will jointly and severally indemnify the escrow agent.
- DEC and TSI shall split the fees and costs of the escrow account and escrow agent.

Part 3: Useful Resources for Students

Dianne Hobbs, Esq, *Drafting and Negotiating Massachusetts Contracts, Chapter 5. Escrow Agreements*, DEMC MA-CLE 5–1 (2013).

Eric C. Surette, *Escrows*, 30A C.J.S. Escrows §§ 1–37 (last updated June 2014).

Terence P. Kennedy, *Ancillary Documents to a Business Purchase Agreement*, 19 DCBA Brief 24 (January 2007).

Escrow Agreements in Mergers and Acquisitions, Executive Legal Summary 391 (last updated Jun. 2014).

CHAPTER 25

EMPLOYMENT AGREEMENT

■ ■ ■

Brief Introduction to Employment Agreements

In many mergers and acquisitions, the buyer will often choose to retain the services of key employees of the selling company and will do so by having those persons execute employment agreements with the buyer. In particular, the buyer may choose to retain those persons who were responsible for the management of or filled other key roles for the selling company. This becomes even more critical when the selling company is a closely held corporation and the owners are intimately involved in the day-to-day management and operations of the selling company.

The employment agreement, while not required to create an employer-employee relationship, establishes the employment relationship in a formal and contractual manner. This agreement is generally used for executives and key employees and not lower level or non-management employees. The employment agreement should address the terms of the employment arrangement between the employer and employee, as well as set forth any pre- or post-employment restrictions imposed on the employee. It is not unusual for the execution of employment agreements by key employees of the seller to be a condition to closing of the transaction.

Part 1: Employment Agreement Drafting Assignment

You are a junior associate at McClelland, Springer & Henderson, LLC, DEC's outside counsel. Melina Chang, the senior associate in charge of the transaction, has tasked you with drafting the employment agreement between DEC and Melissa Green, TSI's current Chief Executive Officer and President. DEC determined that it is in its best interests to have Ms. Green execute a new employment agreement versus revising her current employment agreement with TSI. Ms. Chang has requested that you draft a standard employment agreement containing restrictive provisions regarding confidentiality, non-competition, and non-solicitation. She has requested that you provide her with the initial draft of the employment agreement for her review.

Alternative Assignment: Melina Chang requested that you draft the following provisions of Melissa Green's employment agreement: (i) description of the position and duties; (ii) compensation; (iii) termination rights; and (iv) confidentiality, non-compete, and non-solicitation provisions.

Part 2: Additional Facts for the Assignment

Ms. Chang provided the following additional information to assist you in your preparation of a draft of Ms. Green's employment agreement with DEC:

Melissa Green's base employment details for the new employment agreement with DEC are as follows:

- New title of Senior Vice President.
- $400,000 base salary paid in accordance with DEC's current practices.
- Potential annual bonus of up to 20% of base salary based on achievement of certain net income levels by DEC and subject to the DEC board of directors discretion:
  o Any bonus award will be paid on or before February 15 of the following year.
  o Ms. Green must be employed by DEC on the date that the bonus is paid in order to receive it.
- Standard DEC benefits as are provided to other officers (e.g. health insurance, dental insurance, life insurance of up to $100,000, long-term disability insurance, 401k plan).
- Standard DEC vacation and sick time benefits as are provided to other officers.
- Reimbursement of reasonable out-of-pocket business expenses.
- Subject to annual review and eligibility for a raise in both base salary and bonus potential.
- Initial term of 2 years.

Melissa Green employment duties:

- Ms. Green will be in charge of the operations within the Rocky-Mountain West region.
- Ms. Green will be responsible for overseeing the various locations and for employment decisions within the specified region.
- The regional managers at each location within the specified region will report directly to Ms. Green.
- Ms. Green will be expected to assist in the retention and development of larger customers within the specified region.

- Ms. Green will be expected to periodically travel to the locations within the specified region.
- Ms. Green will have those administrative responsibilities as are assigned to her by the DEC chief operating officer, one of the other DEC executive officers, or the DEC board of directors.
- Ms. Green will have any other additional responsibilities as assigned to her from time-to-time by the DEC chief operating officer or the DEC board of directors.

Additional employment terms:

- DEC will maintain officer and director's insurance coverage on Ms. Green.
- DEC will indemnify Ms. Green in her capacity as a senior vice president with the typical exceptions to such indemnification.
- Ms. Green's entire work product, including the development of all intellectual property, is the sole and exclusive property of DEC.
- Ms. Green and DEC may terminate her employment at any time upon 60 days advance written notice.
- DEC may terminate Ms. Green at any time for cause without advance written notice.
- In the event that Ms. Green is terminated as a result of a change in control of DEC, she is entitled to receive a lump sum payment equal to 1.5 times her then current salary.
- Ms. Green shall keep all confidential and proprietary information regarding DEC confidential during the term of her employment and after her term of employment until such time as the confidential information becomes public through no fault or breach of Ms. Green.
- After her resignation or termination from DEC, Ms. Green shall not accept a position for employment where she directly or indirectly competes with DEC and its business for a period of six months.
- After her resignation or termination from DEC, Ms. Green shall not solicit any other DEC employees for a period of 12 months.
- Any disputes pursuant to this agreement are subject to arbitration in the state of Nevada.
- The agreement may not be assigned by either party without the prior written consent of the other party.

o   DEC may assign the agreement without prior written consent in the event of a change in control.

Part 3: Useful Resources for Students

Part VI. Employment Agreements, Chapter 14. Drafting Employment Contracts, 2 Model Agreements for Corp. Coun. §§ 14:1–14:3 (last updated Feb. 2014).

Part VI. Employment Agreements, Chapter 16. Checklist on Employment Contracts, 2 Model Agreements for Corp. Coun. § 16:1 (last updated Feb. 2014).

Patrick J. Barrett, *Negotiating and Drafting Employment Agreements: Essential Employment Agreement Provisions*, 2012 WL 3058622 (Aug. 2012).

Scott R. Matthews, *Negotiating and Drafting Employment Agreements: Constructing Solid Employment Agreements,* 2012 WL 3058618 (Aug. 2012).

CHAPTER 26

CONSULTING AGREEMENT

■ ■ ■

Brief Introduction to Consulting Agreements

In some merger and acquisition transactions, the buyer may not desire to retain the services of key seller employees for the long-term or those key seller employees may not desire to become employees of the buyer. However, the buyer may wish to retain key seller employees' services for a shorter period of time to more smoothly manage the post-merger transition period. In that scenario, the buyer may enter into a consulting or independent contractor agreement with those seller employees that it views as most critical to the transition process.

The consulting agreement creates a contractual relationship between the buyer and the former employee of the seller to act as a consultant or independent contractor for the buyer. The consulting agreement does not create an employer-employee relationship between the parties and a person should not be retained as a consultant if the person is in essence acting as an employee. The consulting agreement should address the buyer's expectations of the consultant, including a general description of the types of matters the person may be asked to consult about, the amount of hours or time the consultant is expected to dedicate to this role, the amount of pay the consultant will receive, and the term of the consulting arrangement. Similar to employment agreements, the execution of consulting agreements by key seller employees may be a condition to closing of the merger transaction.

Part 1: Consulting Agreement Drafting Assignment

You are a junior associate at McClelland, Springer & Henderson, LLC, DEC's outside counsel. Melina Chang, the senior associate in charge of the transaction, has tasked you with drafting the consulting agreement between DEC and Susan Brown. While DEC desires to have access to Ms. Brown's knowledge of TSI through the post-merger transition period it does not wish to retain her as a long-term employee of DEC nor does Ms. Brown wish to be formally employed by DEC.

Ms. Chang has requested that you draft a standard consulting agreement. It should address the parties' expectations during the transition period, as well as contain restrictive provisions regarding confidentiality, non-solicitation, and intellectual property rights. Ms.

Chang has requested that you provide her with the initial draft of the agreement for her review.

<u>Alternative Assignment</u>: Melina Chang has tasked you with drafting the following provisions of the consulting agreement between DEC and Ms. Shrub: (i) description of the duties and expectations of consultant; (ii) hourly expectations, compensation, and expense reimbursement; (iii) relationship of the parties; and (iv) allowance of other business activities.

Part 2: Additional Facts for the Assignment

Ms. Chang provided the following additional information to assist you in preparing a draft of Susan Brown's consulting agreement:

- Ms. Brown's consulting agreement shall be for an initial term of six months after the closing of the transaction with the option to extend for an additional six months if both parties agree in writing.

- Ms. Brown shall provide up to 25 hours of consulting services per week, but there is no guarantee that DEC will utilize her services for that many hours per week. The parties may mutually agree in writing to exceed the 25 hours per week limitation.

- Ms. Brown will be compensated for her services at the rate of $125/hour. She will be entitled to reimbursement of any reasonable expenses incurred as a result of the consulting arrangement including any local or long-distance travel.

- Ms. Brown shall be an independent contractor and responsible for her own taxes.

- Ms. Brown shall make herself accessible to all executive officers, the board of directors, the auditors, and legal counsel (both inside and outside) of DEC and shall be willing to assist with any questions such parties have regarding TSI's corporate structure, operations, customers, suppliers, employees, outstanding litigation, etc. Ms. Brown shall promptly respond to any requests she receives from these parties and shall do so within two business days of such request.

- Ms. Brown can accept any other work that does not compete with DEC and its business or conflict with her obligations under this contract without notifying or seeking DEC's approval.

- Ms. Brown can accept other work that might compete with DEC and its business upon notification to DEC and receipt of DEC's prior written consent.

- Ms. Brown shall be bound by confidentiality and non-solicitation provisions. Ms. Brown shall keep all confidential information regarding DEC confidential during and after the term of her consulting agreement until such time as the confidential information becomes public through no fault or breach of Ms. Brown. After the conclusion or termination of the consulting agreement, Ms. Brown shall not solicit any DEC employees for a period of 12 months.

- Any work product that Ms. Brown produces pursuant to the consultant relationship, including any intellectual property, shall be the sole and exclusive property of DEC.

- Either party may terminate the consulting agreement without cause upon 30 days prior written notice to the other party. Additionally, DEC can terminate the agreement immediately for cause.

- Neither party may assign the consulting agreement.

Part 3: Useful Resources for Students

Marvin Hyman, *Part 3. Compensating Directors and Officers, Chapter 12. Officer's Compensation—Hiring Executives as Consultants*, 1 Corp. Forms § 12:41 (last updated Jun. 2014).

James H. Walzer, Esq., *Chapter 14. Consultants—General Comments*, 15 N.J. Prac., Legal Forms § 14:1 (4th ed.) (last updated Jul. 2013).

Chapter 44. Guide to Consulting Agreements, 2 Law of Purchasing §§ 44:1–44:71 (2d ed.) (last updated Jan. 2014).

Consulting Agreements Introduction and Overview, 259 Com. L. Adviser Article I (July 2009).

CHAPTER 27

REPRESENTATIONS AND WARRANTIES BRING DOWN CERTIFICATE

■ ■ ■

Brief Introduction to the Representations and Warranties Bring Down Certificate

When the execution of the merger and acquisition agreement and the closing of the transaction do not occur simultaneously, an important condition to the closing of the transaction is for each party to indicate that its representations and warranties in the merger and acquisition agreement are still true and correct as of the closing date of the transaction. This process of reiterating the representations and warranties at the closing date is referred to as a "bring down" condition.

The bring down of the representations and warranties is often satisfied by a company officer executing a certificate that the representations and warranties are still true and correct as of the closing date subject to any relevant qualifying language. The parties to the transaction will expect the officer's certificate to be executed and delivered by the other side as a condition to the closing.

Part 1: Representation and Warranties Bring Down Drafting Assignment

You are a junior associate at Williams & Bowers, PC, TSI's outside counsel. Lisa Goodman, the senior associate managing the TSI transaction, has requested that you prepare a draft of the TSI officer's certificate to bring down the representations and warranties from the date of the execution of the merger and acquisition agreement to the scheduled closing date of the transaction.

Part 2: Additional Facts for the Assignment

In order to prepare the officer's certificate, Ms. Goodman provided you with the following additional information:

- Assume the merger and acquisition agreement was executed on the date of the first class of the semester and that the closing is scheduled to take place two weeks from today's date.

- TSI has continued to operate its business consistent with past practices since executing the merger and acquisition agreement.

Except for the matters discussed below, nothing material has transpired that would impact or prevent the representations and warranties that TSI made in the merger and acquisition agreement from remaining true and correct.

The following matters have occurred since the execution of the merger and acquisition agreement:

- Three larger and five smaller TSI customers opted not to renew their annual contracts. None of these customers indicated that TSI was performing the contracted for services poorly. The customers each indicated that they had located other companies that could undertake the work for significantly lower cost or that they were going to undertake the work themselves. While these customers individually do not represent a material percentage of TSI's revenues, they might be considered a material percentage in the aggregate.

- The pending lawsuit of ABC Management Company against TSI was settled out of court for the sum of $175,000 plus the payment of reasonable attorney's costs and related fees (~$22,000). TSI's insurance carrier covered the costs of the settlement under TSI's business insurance. (See Chapter 9 for additional details).

- The pending lawsuit of Big Golf Course Owner against TSI is proceeding. Big Golf Course Owner is seeking damages of $225,000 plus attorney's fees and costs. TSI and its insurance carrier are continuing efforts to settle the claim. (See Chapter 13 for additional details).

- The employee who had a workers' compensation claim (Sally Dawson), has filed the threatened lawsuit against TSI for emotional distress. She is seeking $500,000 in damages as a result of her fear to walk under trees due to her claimed on-the-job injury. The workers' compensation claim is still pending and the suit for emotional distress was filed three days ago (see Chapter 9 for additional details).

- TSI's revolving line of credit now has an outstanding balance of $246,000 as TSI, in the ordinary course of its business, recently purchased a new truck to replace an older model (see Chapter 9 for additional details).

Part 3: Useful Resources for Students

Alan S. Gutterman, *Part X. Acquisitions and Divestitures, Chapter 291. Buying and Selling a Business—Closing Certificates*, 26 Business Transactions Solutions § 291:39 (last updated July 2014).

Sophie C. Migliazzo, Esq, *Drafting and Negotiating Massachusetts Contracts, Chapter 4. Representations, Warranties, Covenants, and Conditions*, DEMC MA-CLE § 4–1 (2013).

Chapter 2. Taxable Acquisitions in One Step: The Nontax Forms— Warranties, Representations, Covenants, and Conditions— Warranties, Corporate Acquisitions, Mergers and Divestitures § 2:23 (last updated Apr. 2014).

Part II. Guide to Launching and Building Growth—Oriented Companies, Chapter 44. Negotiated Acquisitions, XI. Closing Procedures and Documents—Closing Certificates, Bus. Counselor's Guide to Org. Mgmt. § 44:89 (last updated Jun. 2014).

CHAPTER 28

CLOSING CHECKLIST

■ ■ ■

Brief Introduction to the Closing Checklist

In most merger and acquisition transactions, one or both of the parties should prepare a closing checklist. The closing checklist can be a unified document that is used by all the parties or each side may prepare its own closing checklist. In either circumstance, the checklist should set forth all of the documents that must be drafted and delivered at closing, the party responsible for each document, and any other closing items or actions that must take place in order to complete the transaction. The checklist is generally an evolving document that is updated on a regular basis to indicate where the transaction stands as it moves toward closing. The checklist can be as simple or as detailed as the parties choose, but should ultimately help facilitate the closing of the transaction.

Part 1: Closing Checklist Drafting Assignment

You are a junior associate at Williams & Bowers, PC, TSI's outside counsel. Lisa Goodman, the senior associate managing the TSI transaction, has requested that you prepare a draft of TSI's closing checklist for the transaction. She has indicated that the closing checklist is an internal document that is for the firm and TSI's benefit. The checklist should reflect information regarding the relevant parties to the transaction, the documents already executed, the documents that will be executed at closing, the party responsible for each document, and any other items that must be accomplished and actions that must be taken in order to effectuate the closing of the transaction. In addition, the closing checklist should include information about the status of each document or action listed.

Part 2: Additional Facts for the Assignment

In order to prepare the closing checklist, Ms. Goodman provided you with the following additional information:

Executed documents:

- Confidentiality Agreement.
- Letter of Intent.
- Merger and Acquisition Agreement.

- Hart-Scott-Rodino Filing.

Documents to be executed at closing:

- Assignment of Intellectual Property (*in final form and agreed to by all parties*).
- Escrow Agreement (*in final form and agreed to by all parties*).
- Melissa Green Employment Agreement (*in final negotiation stages*).
- Thomas Shrub Employment Agreement (*in early negotiation stages*).
- Susan Brown Consulting Agreement (*in final negotiation stages*).

TSI action items and documents to be delivered at closing:

- Updated Merger and Acquisition Agreement Disclosure Schedules (*in preparation*).
- Third Party Consents (*in process—all but two received*).
- Contract Assignments (*in process—all but four received*).
- TSI Board of Directors' Unanimous Written Consent Action (*fully executed as of yesterday*).
- TSI Shareholders' Unanimous Written Consent Action (*circulated to all shareholders today for execution*).
- Articles of Merger (*prepared and ready for filing*).
- Certified Good Standing Certificate of TSI (*requested from Secretary of State*).
- Copies of TSI Corporate Governance Documents— Certified Articles of Incorporation, Bylaws, and Meeting Minutes (*prepared and ready for delivery*).
- Updated TSI financial statements—balance sheet and income statement as of most recent month end (*currently being prepared*).
- TSI Secretary's Certificate—certifying validity of corporate governance documents and corporate governance matters (*in final draft form*).
- TSI Officer's Certificate—Representations and Warranties Bring Down (*in final draft form*).
- TSI Board of Directors' Resignation Forms (*all in final draft form*).
- TSI's outside counsel's Legal Opinion (*final language still being negotiated between Williams & Bowers and McClelland, Henderson & Springer*).
- Wiring Instructions (*prepared and ready for delivery*).

Part 3: Useful Resources for Students

E. Thom Rumberger, Jr., Larry S. Adkison, & Elizabeth R. Cobey, *Chapter 12: Closing Mechanics*, The Acquisition and Sale of Emerging Growth Companies: The M&A Exit, 2d ed. (last updated May 2009).

Cathy Krendl, James Krendl, and A Group of Colorado Practice Experts, *Chapter 6. Buying and Selling an Operating Business— Closing and After*, 1 Colo. Prac., Methods of Practice § 6:25 (7th ed.) (last updated May 2014).

CHAPTER 29

CLIENT EMAIL UPDATE

■ ■ ■

Brief Introduction to Client Email Updates

Practicing lawyers communicate with clients in many ways. Some of these types of communication include in person meetings, telephone, virtual online conference, text, or email. It has become more commonplace in the electronic age for lawyers and clients to communicate frequently via email. Email is a quick and easy way for the parties to communicate about day-to-day matters, as well as about larger issues or transactions.

While email messages are often viewed as an informal type of communication, lawyers should still treat the correspondence with a client in a professional manner. Email deserves the same attention to professionalism and detail as any other type of written correspondence with a client. Additionally, as with every type of client communication, both parties must be acutely aware of protecting the attorney-client privilege, as well as protecting the confidentiality of electronically exchanged information.

Part 1: Client Email Update Drafting Assignment

You are a junior associate at Williams & Bowers, PC, TSI's outside counsel. Lisa Goodman, the senior associate managing the TSI transaction, has requested that you prepare a draft of an email to update the TSI Executives regarding the status of the transaction. The email should apprise the TSI Executives of the overall progress of the transaction, including specific details regarding all documents that must be prepared or finalized in order for closing to occur. In addition, Ms. Goodman has asked you to provide the TSI Executives with details regarding the closing of the transaction, including the scheduled time and place. She has requested a draft of the email to review.

Part 2: Additional Facts for the Assignment

In order to prepare the email update, Ms. Goodman provided you with the following additional information:

- You should use the information provided in Chapter 28—Closing Checklist to update the TSI Executives regarding the status of the various transaction related documents and open action items.

- The transaction and closing are proceeding according to schedule and Ms. Goodman does not currently anticipate any material issues or concerns.

- Ms. Goodman would like to schedule an in person meeting with the TSI Executives in the next few business days to discuss all open items and set a time table for their completion.

- The closing is scheduled to take place at the corporate offices of DEC at 9:00 a.m. local time on the last day of the semester.

- DEC has indicated that it will pay travel and lodging costs for one of the TSI Executives to attend the closing, but not for all three.

Part 3: Useful Resources for Students

Anne Enquist & Laurel Oates, *You've Sent Mail: Ten Tips to Take with You to Practice*, 15 No. 2 Perspec. 127 (Winter 2007).

Tracy Turner, *Email Etiquette in the Business World*, 18 No. 1 Perspec. 18 (Fall 2009).

Gerald Lebovits, *E-Mail Netiquette for Lawyers*, 81–DEC N.Y. St. B.J. 64 (November/December 2009).

Janice Mac Avoy, Ivan Espinoza-Madrigal, & Sherita Walton, *Think Twice Before You Hit the Send Button! Practical Considerations in the Use of Email*, 54 No. 6 Prac. Law. 45 (December 2008).

CHAPTER 30

TERMINATION AGREEMENT

■ ■ ■

Brief Introduction to Termination of the Merger and Acquisition Agreement

Most merger and acquisition agreements provide the parties with rights to terminate the agreement upon the occurrence or non-occurrence of specific events. A party may have various unilateral rights to terminate, and in most circumstances, the parties may agree to a mutual termination of the transaction. Termination rights are even more critical when the execution of the merger and acquisition agreement and the closing of the transaction do not occur simultaneously. The parties will want to ensure that they are protected to the greatest extent possible in the circumstance where an event that adversely affects the transaction or parties occurs or a necessary event fails to occur during the gap period.

In the case of a unilateral termination right, the party exercising that right will typically send a letter called a "notice of termination" to the other party that sets forth the reason for the termination and references the relevant section of the merger and acquisition agreement that provides the party with the termination right.

In the case of mutually agreed upon termination, the parties generally enter into a "termination agreement." This agreement will set forth (i) the reason for the termination; (ii) the provision in the merger and acquisition agreement that allows for the agreed upon termination; (iii) how expenses and termination fees will be divided between the parties; and (iv) various other standard and miscellaneous provisions.

Part 1: Termination Agreement Drafting Assignment

DEC and TSI have mutually agreed to terminate the merger and acquisition transaction. You are a junior associate at McClelland, Springer & Henderson, LLC, DEC's outside counsel. Melina Chang, the senior associate in charge of the DEC transaction, has asked you to draft the mutual termination agreement between the parties. She has indicated that DEC and TSI are in complete agreement about proceeding with the mutual termination of the transaction and would like a standard mutual termination agreement.

Part 2: Additional Facts for the Assignment

In order to prepare the termination agreement, Ms. Chang provided you with the following additional information:

- The termination agreement will be effective as of one week from today's date.

- The merger and acquisition agreement was executed on the date of the first class of the semester.

- The transaction is being terminated because the parties have concluded that all of the conditions required to close the transaction cannot be satisfied.

- The board of directors of both DEC and TSI believe it is in the best interests of their respective companies to terminate the transaction.

- Assume the transaction is being terminated pursuant to Section 9.01 of the merger and acquisition agreement.

- As a result of the termination, all the rights and obligations of the parties shall cease and neither party shall suffer any liability.

- Even though the agreement to terminate is mutual, DEC was the party that initiated the termination discussions and as such, assume that pursuant to Section 11.09 of the merger and acquisition agreement, DEC is required to pay up to a maximum of $25,000 of TSI's legal fees and expenses relating to the transaction. TSI must submit proof of such legal fees and expenses within five business days of execution of the termination agreement and DEC shall reimburse TSI within ten business days of receipt of such proof.

- DEC shall be responsible for any and all costs pertaining to the Hart-Scott-Rodino filing that was in process at the time of the decision to terminate.

- Other than as set forth above, each party shall bear its own costs and expenses related to the transaction.

- Neither party owes any termination or break-up fees to the other party as a result of this mutual termination.

Part 3: Useful Resources for Students

Judd F. Sneirson, *Merger Agreements, Termination Fees, and the Contract-Corporate Tension*, 2002 Colum. Bus. L. Rev. 573 (2002).

Alan S. Gutterman, *Part X. Acquisitions and Divestitures, Chapter 291. Buying and Selling Businesses—Termination*, 26 Business Transactions Solutions § 291:27 (last updated July 2014).

CHAPTER 31

PRESS RELEASE

■ ■ ■

Brief Introduction to the Press Release

In the context of a merger and acquisition transaction between two private entities, there is often no statutory obligation to issue a press release, make a public announcement, or submit a filing regarding the acquisition. However, the buyer and seller may want to publicly announce the transaction so that those parties who might be interested are alerted to the fact that it has been completed. In particular, the buyer and seller may want shareholders, customers, suppliers, and other entities operating within the industry to know about the transaction.

One of the primary reasons to publish a press release is to inform the general public and the stakeholders of the companies about the news and to prevent the circulation of false or inaccurate information regarding the transaction. The press release should convey the pertinent details of the transaction in a clear and succinct manner. It should be written in a professional business voice, omitting legalese, and should convey how the transaction will impact the future of both companies.

Part 1: Press Release Drafting Assignment

(For purposes of this assignment, assume the parties did not terminate the merger per Chapter 30).

You are a junior associate at McClelland, Springer & Henderson, LLC, DEC's outside counsel. Wil Henderson, the partner in charge of certain aspects of the transaction, has tasked you with drafting the press release that will announce the merger of TSI with and into the new DEC subsidiary, TSINI.

Mr. Henderson has indicated that the press release should state the relevant facts of the transaction and should express that both DEC and TSI view this as an overwhelmingly positive development for both companies and each company's respective stakeholders. He has also indicated that the press release should include at least two quotes from company representatives at each of DEC and TSI. Mr. Henderson has requested that you prepare and submit a draft of the press release to him for his review.

Part 2: Additional Facts for the Assignment

Students should refer to the information learned from the letter of intent assignment (see Chapter 4), the merger assignment (see Chapter 7), and the merger consideration assignment (see Chapter 8) for pertinent facts and details regarding the terms of the transaction between DEC, the newly formed DEC subsidiary, TSINI, and TSI.

Mr. Henderson has provided you with the following additional information to assist you in preparing the press release:

- The issuance date for the press release will be one week from today's date.
- DEC's marketing department will issue the press release and the contact information is as follows:

Dutch Elm Company
10000 Patrick Lane
Las Vegas, NV 89118
www.dec.com
Kylie Star, Vice President of Marketing Communications
kstar@dec.com
702-555-5555

Each Company's tag line is as follows:

- DEC is one of the leading providers of premiere landscape maintenance services in the continental United States. DEC has over 3,500 customers nation-wide. Its website is www.dec.com.
- TSI is the preeminent provider of commercial landscaping services in the state of Colorado. TSI has over 250 customers in the state. Its website is www.tsi.com.

DEC Company Representative Quotes (*or students can create their own quotes*):

- Michelle Smith, Senior Vice President of Sales & Marketing: "The merger of TSI into DEC's newly formed subsidiary and the securing of TSI's customers enables DEC to establish a strong presence in the state of Colorado. As a result, DEC will grow its market share and presence in Colorado immediately and be positioned for greater success in the Midwest."
- Bernard Thompson, Chief Operating Officer: "TSI's well-established business and customer relationships afford us immediate entry into the marketplace. We can hit the ground running and further establish DEC as the premier provider of landscaping services in the Midwest."

- Fred Wilcox, Chief Executive Officer and President: "We are thrilled about the TSI merger and the hiring of Melissa Green as part of the DEC management team. Melissa brings a wealth of experience and expertise to the business operations and long-standing relationships that TSI has in the Colorado community. She will help enable a smooth transition."

TSI Company Representative Quotes (*or students can create their own quotes*):

- Melissa Green, Chief Executive Officer and President: "By merging TSI into DEC's subsidiary and joining the DEC management team, we can more effectively serve our Colorado customers. Not only will our customers continue to receive the quality service they have come to expect, but they will now have the opportunity to consider and invest in new services that are available as a result of this merger."

- Susan Brown, Senior Vice President and Secretary: "What an exciting time for TSI and its customers—by joining forces with DEC we are expanding our ability to grow and cement our customer relationships. With the planned seamless transition, our customers will not experience any disruption in their services and will only see the added benefits."

- Thomas Shrub, Chief Financial Officer: "TSI's decision to enter into the merger with DEC was a wise decision. Melissa and I will remain an integral part of the consolidated operations and TSI's customers will continue to receive quality service. It is a win-win situation for both companies as well as the customers of TSI."

Part 3: Useful Resources for Students

Part E. Corporate Operations and Planning, Chapter 13. Public Relations and Advertising—How to Prepare a Press Release, Mod. Corp. Checklists § 13:8 (last updated May 2014).

Alan J. Berkely, *ALI-ABA Course of Study—Some FAQs and Answers About Corporate Disclosure*, SP057 ALI-ABA 341 (2009).

APPENDIX A

LIST OF PERSONS AND PARTIES WITH RELATED DEFINITIONS

■ ■ ■

Tree Services, Inc.

ABC Management Company (ABC): TSI customer that has sued TSI as a result of damages from a dropped tree limb.

Big Bank: TSI's commercial lender.

Big Golf Course Owner: TSI customer that has sued TSI as a result of the removal and damage of trees at various golf courses.

Rolland Brown: Outside Director.

Susan Brown: A founder of TSI, and Senior Vice President and Secretary.

Sally Dawson: TSI employee who has filed a workers' compensation claim and is threatening an emotional distress action against TSI.

Dunton & Teller, LLC: TSI's Public Accountants/Auditors.

Giant Real Estate Company: TSI's landlord for its commercial space.

Lisa Goodman: Senior Attorney at William & Bowers, PC and lead attorney for the merger and acquisition transaction.

Melissa Green: A founder of TSI, Chief Executive Officer and President, and Chairperson of the Board of Directors.

Michael Lewis: Senior Vice President of Finance.

Erin Mooney: Outside Director.

Nevada State Bank: The escrow agent for the merger and acquisition transaction.

Jonathon Nixon: Outside Director.

Thomas Shrub: A founder of TSI, Chief Financial Officer, and an Inside Director.

Margaret Smith: Partner at Dunton & Teller, LLC and partner in charge of the TSI account.

Thorny Shrubs, Inc.: Colorado company that appears to be infringing TSI's trademark.

Tree Services, Inc. (TSI or Seller): The selling entity in the merger and acquisition transaction, 6789 120th Street, Commerce City, CO 80022.

TSI Executives: Melissa Green, Thomas Shrub, and Susan Brown, collectively.

Webmasters Limited: TSI's website developer.

Williams & Bowers, PC: TSI's outside counsel located at 2200 Thirtieth Avenue, Suite 8900, Denver, CO 80202, (720) 555-5555 (phone), (720) 555-5556 (facsimile).

Bryan Williams: Partner at Williams & Bowers, PC and managing partner for the merger and acquisition transaction.

Dutch Elm Company

William Carlton: Outside Director

Melina Chang: Senior Attorney at McClelland, Springer & Henderson, LLC and lead attorney for the merger and acquisition transaction.

Richard Clark: DEC's account manager at Northern Bank.

Dutch Elm Company (DEC or Buyer): The buying entity in the merger and acquisition transaction, 10000 Patrick Lane, Las Vegas, Nevada 89118.

Margaret Fife: A founder of DEC, Chief Financial Officer, and an Inside Director.

FS Capital: Venture capital firm that invested in DEC and owns DEC common stock.

Wil Henderson: Partner at McClelland, Springer & Henderson, LLC handling certain aspects of the merger and acquisition transaction.

Harold Jenson: Outside Director.

Robert Lawson: Vice President and Secretary.

McClelland, Springer & Henderson, LLC: DEC's outside counsel located at 5555 Rampart Ridge Road, Suite 55, Las Vegas, NV 89117, (702) 555-5555 (phone), (702) 555-5550 (facsimile).

Jeffrey McClelland: Partner at McClelland, Springer & Henderson, LLC and managing partner for the merger and acquisition transaction.

Lisa Montgomery: Outside Director.

Nevada State Bank: The escrow agent for the merger and acquisition transaction.

Northern Bank: DEC's commercial bank and commercial lender.

Pierce & Conway, LLC: DEC's Public Accountants/Auditors.

<u>Maria Samuel</u>: Partner at Pierce & Conway, LLC and partner in charge of the DEC account.

<u>Michelle Smith</u>: Senior Vice President of Sales & Marketing.

<u>Maria Snyder</u>: Partner at Pierce & Conway, LLC and partner in charge of DEC account.

<u>Zoie Springer</u>, Partner at McClelland, Springer & Henderson, LLC handling the due diligence investigation of TSI for the merger and acquisition transaction.

<u>Bernard Thompson</u>: A founder of DEC, Chief Operating Officer, and an Inside Director.

<u>TSI NEWCO, Inc. (TSINI)</u>: A Nevada C Corporation and the newly formed wholly owned subsidiary of DEC.

<u>Susan Watertown</u>: Outside Director.

<u>Fred Wilcox</u>: A founder of DEC, Chief Executive Officer and President, and Chairperson of the Board of Directors.

APPENDIX B

DUE DILIGENCE DOCUMENTS

■ ■ ■

**Commercial Lease Agreement Between
Tree Services, Inc. and Giant Real Estate Company**

Commercial Lease Agreement[1]

This Commercial Lease Agreement (the "Lease Agreement") is made as of this 1st day of April, 2004 between Tree Services, Inc., a Colorado corporation, whose address is 6789 120th Street, Commerce City, CO 80022 (the "Lessee") and Giant Real Estate Company, a Colorado limited liability company with an address at 55555 Tower Road, Brighton, CO 80022 (the "Lessor).

WITNESSETH:

For and in consideration of the rental herein reserved, and of the covenants, conditions, agreements, and stipulations of the Lessee hereinafter expressed, the parties agree as follows:

1. Premises. The Lessor hereby leases to Lessee, and Lessee hereby leases from Lessor, the following described premises: 6789 120th Street, Units A–C, Commerce City, Colorado 80022

    (a) Being a portion of the commercial building located at 6789 120th Street in Commerce City, as shown on the schematic attached hereto marked Exhibit A, and by reference made a part hereof, containing approximately 6,000 square feet, hereinafter referred to as "Premises."

    (b) Together with the right to use in common with Lessor, its employees, invitees, and customers, and Lessor's other tenants and their employees, invitees, and customers, the parking areas provided by the Lessor, its successors, or assigns, in the designated areas for the parking of automobiles, which are contiguous to the building in which the Premises are located; provided that the Lessor retains the right to make reasonable rules and regulations with reference to the use of said parking area, including the right to provide for certain reserved parking as, from time to time, determined by the Lessor, and particularly provided that employees, agents, and principals of Lessee shall park in designated areas so as to assure Lessor's other tenants and Lessor's customers and visitors convenient and proximate parking contiguous to the building or buildings in which its tenants are located.

---

[1] This contract was adapted from *Form—Office Lease Agreement (Simple)*, 4 Commercial Real Estate Forms 3d §13:7.

(c) Lessee acknowledges that: (1) except for the work to be performed on the attached Exhibit B (if any), Lessee has inspected the Premises and hereby accepts same in an "as is" condition, and (2) Lessor has made no warranties and/or representations regarding the condition of the Premises.

2. Term.

(a) The initial term of this Lease shall be for five (5) years commencing on June 1, 2004 and terminating on the May 31, 2009 and shall automatically renew for one (1) additional five (5) year term unless either party notifies the other of their intent to terminate the Lease in writing on or before one hundred twenty (120) days prior to the end of the initial lease term. Notwithstanding the foregoing, the parties may mutually choose to renew the Lease for additional terms and such renewals must be in writing signed by both parties.

(b) Any holding over after the expiration of the term hereof, or of any renewal other than the ones stipulated in section 2(a), shall be construed to be a tenancy from month to month, at a monthly rental at 175% greater than the monthly rental applicable to the rent due for the last month under this Lease Agreement.

(c) During the final six (6) months of this Lease term, Lessor shall be permitted to show prospective tenants the Premises upon giving Lessee two hours' notice.

3. Rental. Lessee hereby covenants and agrees to pay to the Lessor at 55555 Tower Road, Brighton, CO 80022, or at such other place as the Lessor may from time to time designate in writing, as rental for said Premises during the term of this Lease, an annual rental, payable monthly in advance, beginning on the first day of commencement of this Lease and continuing on the same day of each month thereafter for the entire term of this Lease as follows:

(a) $2,200 per month for the first twelve months of this Lease;

(b) $2,275 per month for the second twelve months of this Lease;

(c) $2,350 per month for the third twelve months of this Lease; and

(d) $2,500 per month for every month after the completion of the third twelve-month period.

(e)   as additional rent, 10% (Lessee's pro rata share) of any and all increases in Real Estate Taxes, as hereinafter defined, above those for the fiscal tax year commencing on the 1st day of June, 2014 (hereinafter referred to as the Base Tax Year) imposed on the land and buildings of which the Premises forms a part with respect to every calendar year or part thereof during the term of this lease, whether any such increase results from a higher tax rate or an increase in the assessed valuation of the property, or both. Real Estate Taxes shall be defined as including the following items: (i) real estate taxes, (ii) assessments levied, assessed, or imposed against such land and/or buildings or the rents or profits therefrom to the extent that the same shall be in lieu of all or any portion of any items hereinabove set forth, and (iii) all water and sewer rents, charges, taxes, and frontage assessed or imposed. If due to a change in the method of taxation, any franchise, income, profit, or other tax, however designated, shall be levied against Lessor's interest in the property in whole or in part for or in lieu of any tax which would otherwise constitute Real Estate Taxes, such taxes shall be included in the term Real Estate Taxes for purposes hereof. All such payments shall be approximately prorated for any partial calendar years in which the term of this lease shall commence or expire. A copy of the tax bill shall be sufficient evidence of the amount of Real Estate Taxes.

Only Lessor shall be eligible to institute tax reduction or other proceedings to reduce the assessed valuation of the land and buildings. Should Lessor be successful in any such reduction proceedings and obtain a rebate for periods during which Lessee has paid its share of increases, and provided that Lessee is not in default in payment of rent or additional rent due under this lease, Lessor shall, after deducting its expenses, including, without limitation, attorney's fees and disbursements in connection therewith, promptly return Lessee's pro rata share of such rebate after Lessor has received such proceeds. Lessee may not obtain any portion of the benefits that may accrue to Lessor from any reduction in Real

Estate Taxes for any year below those imposed in the Base Tax Year.

Along with notification of any increases in Real Estate Taxes for which the Lessor requests payment from Lessee, Lessor shall also furnish (i) a copy of the current tax bill, (ii) a copy of the tax bill for the base year, (iii) a statement showing calculation of Lessee's proportionate share of the increase in Real Estate Taxes for which payment is being requested in sufficient detail to enable Lessee to verify the accuracy of the amount it is being requested to pay. Failure by the Lessor to provide notification of and the supporting documentation listed above of Lessee's proportionate share of increases in Real Property Taxes within thirty (30) days after the due date of the current year's tax bill shall constitute a permanent and irrevocable waiver by the Lessor of Lessee's obligation to pay said increase in Real Estate Taxes for the corresponding tax year.

(f)   a sum equal to 5% of any fixed or additional rent not received by Lessor within ten (10) days of the due date thereof.

4.   Security Deposit. The Lessee shall deposit with the Lessor on or before the 1st day of June, 2004, the sum of $4,500 in cash as security for the payment of the rent provided herein and for the observance and performance by the Lessee of all of the terms, provisions, and conditions of this Lease on its part to be kept and performed; and further to indemnify the Lessor for any loss, costs, fees, and expenses which the Lessor may incur by reason of any default by the Lessee. The Lessor shall repay to the Lessee the security deposit or any balance thereof upon the termination or expiration of the term of this Lease or any extension thereof, by crediting the same on account of payment of the rent for the 1st month of the Lease or additional term, as the case may be. In the event of any failure in the payment of rent or other sum, or of any default by the Lessee in the performance of the terms, provisions, and conditions of this Lease, the Lessor shall have the right to apply the security deposit against any loss, costs, fees, and expenses caused thereby. The security deposit shall bear no interest.

5. Use of Premises. The Lessee shall use said premises for its commercial landscape business operations and office and for no other purpose whatsoever.

Lessee shall comply with all present and future laws or ordinances applicable to the Premises and shall not commit or suffer waste on the premises, or use or permit anything on the premises which may be illegal, or constitute a private or public nuisance, or conflict with or invalidate or increase the cost of any of Lessor's fire and extended coverage insurance, or which may be dangerous to persons or the property of the Lessor or other tenants of Lessor's building, their agents, servants, employees, and customers. Notwithstanding the foregoing, Lessee's effecting an increase in the cost of any of Lessor's fire and extended insurance is curable by Lessee's payment of such increase in cost.

6. Repairs, Maintenance, and Changes by Lessee

(a) The Lessor shall make all necessary repairs to the interior of the Premises, including window and plate glass and the fixtures and equipment therein or used in connection therewith, including the maintenance of all fixtures and equipment located within the Premises, which repairs shall be in quality and class equal to the original work, in order to maintain said premises, fixtures, and equipment in good condition and repair; provided, however, that the Lessee shall be responsible for any painting, carpeting, or any repair necessitated by the Lessee's neglect or omission. If Lessee fails to perform its obligations of maintenance or repair hereunder, Lessor is authorized to come onto the Premises, make such repairs, and upon billing to the Lessee by the Lessor, Lessee shall reimburse the Lessor for the costs of such repairs plus interest thereon at the lesser of the highest legal rate allowed in the State of Colorado or 5 points above the prime rate of interest charged by the Wells Fargo Bank or its successor in the State of Colorado. Upon the expiration of or prior termination of this Lease, the Lessee shall remove all property of the Lessee from the premises, except plumbing and other fixtures and leasehold improvements which may have been installed by the Lessee and except as otherwise provided in this Lease, and surrender the Premises to the Lessor in as good order and condition as they were upon Lessee commencing business, or were placed by Lessee thereafter. Lessee shall be responsible for repairing all "wear and tear" caused by Lessee prior to surrendering the premises. Any property left on the premises after the expiration or other termination of this Lease may be disposed of by Lessor in any manner and without any liability to the Lessee.

(b) The Lessee shall not make any changes, alteration, additions, or improvements to the Premises without the written consent of the Lessor, which consent may be withheld in Lessor's sole and absolute discretion. The Lessee is required to furnish and use floor mats under all chairs behind desks.

(c) The Lessor shall maintain the plumbing and heating lines; however, all repairs to the plumbing and heating lines necessitated by the action of the Lessee or the Lessee's agents or employees shall be at the expense of the Lessee.

(d) Lessee, at its sole cost and expense, shall regularly monitor the Premises for the presence of mold or any conditions that reasonably can be expected to give rise to mold and shall promptly notify the Lessor in writing if Lessee suspects mold at the Premises.

7. Utilities. All electric light, heat, power, sewerage, fuel, and other utility service charges and assessments (excepting water) shall be paid by the Lessee for the benefit of the Premises; and Lessor shall only provide and pay for all water for drinking and lavatory purposes. All water consumed by Lessee for other purposes shall be paid for by Lessee, and Lessor shall install, at Lessor's sole cost and expense, a water meter to measure such excess consumption. Lessor shall be permitted to inspect the Premises from time to time to assure that Lessee is complying with this provision. Lessor may install, at Lessor's sole cost and expense, a security system to monitor the Premises. If Lessor elects to install such system, Lessor may invoice Lessee the monthly cost of utilizing the system, which Lessee must pay within five (5) business days of receipt of the invoice.

8. Janitorial Services. Lessee agrees to keep all rubbish and garbage in containers while on the Premises and shall dispose of all of such rubbish and garbage in the

dumpster or other containers provided by Lessor and located at the west side of the Premises.

The Lessee shall perform and provide for all of Lessee's janitorial services required on the Premises; however, Lessee agrees to use the janitorial service used or suggested by Lessor for such period of time if the cost of such services is reasonable and its services are of reasonable quality.

9. Damage to Lessee's Property or Premises.

   (a) The Lessor and its agents shall not be liable in damages, by abatement in rent or otherwise, for any damage either to the person or the property of the Lessee, or for the loss of or damage to any property of the Lessee by theft or from any other cause whatsoever, whether similar or dissimilar to the foregoing. The Lessor or its agents shall not be liable for any injury or damage to persons or property, or loss or interruption to business resulting from fire, explosion, falling plaster, steam, gas, electricity, water, rain, snow, or leaks from any part of the building, or from the pipes, appliances, or plumbing works, or from the roof, street, or subsurface, or from any other place, or by dampness, or by any cause of whatsoever nature; nor shall the Lessor or its agents be liable for any damage caused by other tenants or persons in said building, or caused by operations in construction of any private or public or quasi-public work. None of the limitations of the liability of Lessor or its agents provided for in this subsection (a) shall apply if such loss, injury, or damages are proximately caused by the gross negligence or breach by the Lessor, its agents, employees, or independent contractors.

   (b) Lessee's Liability for Damage to Lessor's Property. The Lessee shall be liable for any damage to the building or property therein which may be caused by its act or negligence, or the acts of his agents, employees, or customers, and the Lessor may, at its option, repair such damage, and the said Lessee shall thereupon reimburse and compensate the Lessor as additional rent, within five (5) days after rendition of a statement by the Lessor, for the total cost of such repair and damage, except as hereinafter provided in Item 10(d).

10. Indemnity, Liability Insurance, Building Insurance, Waiver of Subrogation

   (a) The Lessee hereby indemnifies and agrees to hold the Lessor harmless and free from damages sustained by person or property, and against all claims of third persons for damages arising out of the Lessee's use of the Premises, and for all damages and monies paid out by Lessor in settlement of any claim or judgments, as well as for all expenses and attorney's fees incurred in connection therewith.

   (b) Lessee shall, during the entire term of this Lease and any renewal hereof, keep in full force and effect a policy of public liability and property damage insurance with respect to the Premises, and the business operated by Lessee.

   (c) Lessor, at its sole cost and expense, agrees to keep the building and improvements (including the Premises) insured against loss or damage by fire or other casualty insurable under standard fire and extended coverage insurance in an amount equal to the full current replacement cost of said building(s).

   (d) Lessor agrees, to the extent it is then obtainable from any financially responsible insurance company, that its insurance policies for fire and extended coverage covering the building and the proposed property fixtures and equipment located thereon or therein belonging to Lessor, will contain in substance the following endorsement: "This insurance shall be invalidated should the insured waive, in writing prior to a loss, any or all right of recovery against any party for the loss occurring to the property described herein." Provided such endorsement is obtained, Lessor agrees that it will not make any claim against, or seek to recover from, Lessee for any loss or damage to the building and/or the personal property fixtures and equipment of Lessor located thereon or therein, by such fire or the perils of the extended coverage insurance within the scope of the aforesaid policies, whether or not the loss or damage is due to carelessness or negligence of Lessee, its servants, agents, and employees. If, as a condition of making the aforesaid endorsement available to it, the insurance carriers of Lessor shall require the payment of an additional premium over and above the normal and standard premiums for the coverage involved, Lessor will notify Lessee to such effect, and if Lessee shall require that the endorsement be contained in Lessor's policies, then Lessee shall pay such additional premium cost.

11. Damage or Destruction to Premises

    (a) If the Premises, or any portion thereof, shall be damaged during the term by fire or any casualty insurable under the standard fire and extended coverage insurance policies, but are not wholly untenantable, the Lessor shall repair and/or rebuild the same as promptly as possible, provided that the proceeds from Lessor's insurance policies are available to Lessor. The Lessor shall not be required to repair or rebuild any fixtures, installations, improvements, or leasehold improvements made to the interior of the Premises by Lessee, nor Lessee's exterior signs. Such repairs and/or replacements are to be made by Lessee. In such event, the Lease shall not terminate, but shall remain in full force and effect, and a proportionate reduction in the fixed minimum monthly rental shall be made from the time of such fire or casualty until said Premises are repaired or restored, except (i) if the Lessee can use and occupy the Premises without substantial inconvenience; or (ii) if said repairs are delayed at the request or by reason of any act on the part of the Lessee which prevents or delays the repair of said Premises by Lessor, there shall be no reduction in rental while said Premises are being repaired, nor for any period of delay caused by or requested by Lessee. Lessor's obligation to repair shall be subject to any delays from labor troubles, material shortages, insurance claim negotiations, or any other causes, whether similar or dissimilar to the foregoing, beyond Lessor's control.

    (b) If the Premises are rendered wholly untenantable by fire or other cause, or if the Premises or the building in which they are located should be damaged or destroyed by fire or other casualty, to the extent of 75% or more of the monetary value of either thereof, whether the Premises themselves be damaged or not, or so that 50% or more of the floor space contained in either thereof shall be rendered untenantable, then, and in that event, Lessor may, at its option, terminate this Lease or elect to repair or rebuild the same. If, as a result of any damage either to the Premises or to the building of which they are a part, the Lessor determines to demolish or rebuild the Premises, or the building of which they are a part, then, and in any such event, the Lessor may also terminate this Lease. In any of the foregoing instances, the Lessor shall notify the Lessee as to its election within ninety (90) days after the casualty in question. If the Lessor elects to terminate this Lease, then the same shall terminate ninety (90) days after such notice is given, and the Lessee shall immediately vacate the Premises and surrender the same to the Lessor, paying the rent to the time of such vacation and surrender, subject to an equitable abatement from the time of said damage. If the Lessor does not elect to terminate this Lease, the Lessor shall repair and/or rebuild the Premises as promptly as possible, subject to any delay from causes beyond its reasonable control, and the term shall continue in full force and effect, subject to equitable abatement in the fixed minimum monthly rental from the time of said damage or destruction until said Premises are repaired or restored.

12. Eminent Domain. If the Premises, or any part thereof, shall be taken under eminent domain proceedings, or transferred to a public authority in lieu of such proceedings, Lessor may terminate this Lease as of the date when possession is taken. All damages awarded for such taking shall belong to and be the property of Lessor. Lessee shall have no claim against Lessor by reason of such taking or termination and shall not have any claim or right to any portion of the amount that may be awarded or paid to Lessor as a result of any such taking, except that Lessee shall have the right to make a claim against such public authority for its loss of business and for any other relief available to Lessee by law in the event such taking involves the physical taking of all or a portion of the Premises, and, in such event, Lessee shall also have the right to terminate this Lease as of the date when possession is taken by the public authority.

13. Estoppel Certificate Statement, Attornment, Subordination, and Execution of Documents.

    (a) Lessee agrees that at any time and from time to time at reasonable intervals, within five (5) business days after written request by Lessor, Lessee will execute, acknowledge, and deliver to Lessor, Lessor's mortgagee, or others designated by Lessor, a certificate in such form as may from time to time be provided, ratifying this Lease and certifying:

(i) that this Lease is in full force and effect, and has not been assigned, modified, supplemented, or amended in any way or that there has been an assignment, modification, supplement, or amendment, identifying the same;

(ii) that this Lease represents the entire agreement between Lessor and Lessee as to the subject matter hereof any assignment, modification, supplement, or amendment, identifying the same;

(iii) the Commencement Date and Termination Date;

(iv) that all conditions under this Lease to be performed by Lessor have been satisfied (and if not, what conditions remain unperformed);

(v) that to the knowledge of the signer of such writing, no default exists in the enforcement of this Lease by Lessor or specifying each default, defense, or offset of which the signer may have knowledge;

(vi) that no rental has been paid in advance other than for the month in which such certificate is signed by Lessee;

(vii) the amount of the security deposited with Lessor pursuant to Item 4 hereof; and

(viii) the date to which all rentals due hereunder have been paid under this Lease.

(a) Lessee shall, in the event any proceedings are brought for the foreclosure of, or in the event of exercise of the power of sale under any mortgage covering the Premises, attorn to the purchaser upon any such foreclosure or sale and recognize such purchaser as the Lessor, subject to all of Lessee's duties, obligations, rights, and options under this Lease.

(b) Upon request by the Lessor, Lessee shall subordinate its rights hereunder to the lien of any mortgage or mortgages, or the lien resulting from any other method of financing or refinancing, now or hereafter in force against the land and/or the buildings of which the Premises are a part, or against any buildings hereafter placed upon the land of which the Premises are a part, and to all advances made or hereafter to be made upon the security thereof; provided, however, that a condition precedent to Lessee's requirement to subordinate hereunder shall be that Lessee, upon any default in the terms of such financing by Lessor, shall have the right to pay the rental due hereunder directly to the mortgagee or other persons to whom Lessor may be obligated under such financing and, as long as Lessee does so pay the rentals as herein provided, this Lease and all Lessee's rights and options hereunder shall remain in full force and effect as to such mortgagee or other financing obligee of Lessor.

(c) The Lessee, upon request of any party in interest, shall execute, within five (5) business days of Lessee's receipt, such instruments or certificates to carry out the intent of these paragraphs above as shall be requested by the Lessor. Provided, however, that nothing contained in such instruments or certificates required by Lessor shall be in derogation of any rights granted to Lessee hereunder, nor expand Lessee's obligations hereunder, and if any such instruments or certificates would have the effect of accomplishing one or both of the foregoing, either explicitly or implicitly, then Lessee shall not be obligated to execute the same.

14. Default.

(a) If the Lessee shall, at any time, be in default of the payment of either rent or any payments required of Lessee hereunder or any part thereof, for more than five (5) days after the same shall be due hereunder, regardless of whether demand has been made therefor, or if Lessee shall be in default of any of the other covenants and conditions of this Lease to be kept, observed, and performed by Lessee for more than fifteen (15) days after the giving of written notice by the Lessor to the Lessee of such default, or if Lessee shall vacate or abandon the Premises, or fail to take possession of the Premises and actively operate its business therein, or if Lessee shall be adjudged a bankrupt, or if a receiver or trustee shall be appointed and shall not be discharged within thirty (30) days from the date of such appointment, then and in any such events the Lessor may re-enter the Premises by summary proceedings or otherwise, and thereupon may expel all persons and remove all property therefrom, without becoming liable to prosecution therefor, and may, among other remedies, elect:

(i)   To relet said Premises as the agent of the Lessee, and reserve the rent therefrom, applying the same first to the payment of the reasonable expense of such re-entry, and then to the payment of the rent accruing hereunder; but whether or not the Premises are relet, the Lessee shall remain liable for the equivalent of all rent and other charges provided for under this Lease, plus the cost of reletting, if any, which said amount shall be due and payable to the Lessor as damages, or rent, as the case may be, on the successive monthly rent days hereinabove provided; or

(ii)   To terminate this Lease and immediately resume possession of the Premises, wholly discharged from any obligations under the term of this lease, and may re-enter and repossess said Premises, free from any and all claims on the part of the Lessee. Termination of the Lease does not discharge or in any way affect Lessee's obligation to pay Lessor all the rents or other charges or payments accruing under the Lease up to the date of termination.

(b)   Lessor shall not be in default unless it fails to perform the obligations required of Lessor by this Lease Agreement within sixty (60) days after written notice by Lessee to Lessor specifying which obligation(s) Lessor has failed to perform. Provided, however, that if the nature of the specified obligation(s) is such that more than sixty (60) days are required for performance, then Lessor shall not be in default if it commences performance within such sixty (60)-day period and thereafter diligently prosecutes the same to completion. If Lessor has not cured or commenced to cure the default set forth in said notice within said sixty (60)-day period, Lessee may at its option either (i) cure such default and deduct the reasonable costs and expenses incurred from the next and succeeding rent payment(s) or (ii) cancel this Lease and, in such event, this Lease shall thereupon cease, terminate, and come to an end with the same force and effect as though the original demised term had expired at that time.

15. Subletting and Assigning. The Lessee shall not sublet any portion of the Premises nor assign this Lease in whole or in part without the written consent of the Lessor as to both the terms of such assignment or sublease and the identity of such assignee or sublessee, which consent shall not unreasonably be withheld, and in the event of a subletting so approved by Lessor, Lessee shall nevertheless remain obligated to Lessor under the terms of this Lease Agreement.

16. Signs. The Lessee shall not install nor maintain any sign anywhere on the property constituting the Premises whether neon, translucent, plastic, or otherwise, unless plans and specifications shall first be submitted to Lessor in writing, and the Lessor shall have the right, in its sole discretion, to direct and determine the size, content, design, construction, and location of such sign on the Premises.

17. Quiet Enjoyment. The Lessor covenants and agrees with the Lessee that upon the Lessee paying the said rent and performing all the covenants and conditions aforesaid on the Lessee's part to be observed and performed, the Lessee shall and may peaceably and quietly have, hold, and enjoy the Premises hereby leased, for the term aforesaid; subject, however, to the terms of this Lease, any mortgage, or other instruments now or hereafter created by the Lessor.

18. Memorandum of Lease. Lessee agrees that it will not record this Lease or otherwise make it a matter of public record unless required in any litigation involving Lessee. If the Lessee or Lessor request, the parties will enter into a short form lease, describing the Premises and the term of this Lease, and including any other terms necessary to permit the recording of such short form lease. Such recording, if requested by Lessee, shall be at its cost and expense.

19. Notices. All notices to be given under this Lease shall be in writing and shall either be served personally or sent by

certified mail, return receipt requested. All notices mailed as herein provided shall be deemed received three (3) days after mailing. Notices to Lessor shall be sent to the address set forth in the preamble hereof or such other address as the Lessor may specify in written notice to Lessee. Notices to Lessee shall be sent to the mailing address of the Premises, or such other addresses as the Lessee may specify in written notice to Lessor. Lessor agrees that any notices received from Tree Services, Inc. shall be deemed official communication from Lessee.

20. Interest. Any amount due from Lessee to Lessor under this Lease which is not paid when due shall bear interest at the lesser of the highest legal rate allowed in the State of Colorado or five (5) points above the prime rate of interest charged by Wells Fargo Bank or its successor in Colorado from the date due until paid; provided, however, the payment of such interest shall not excuse or cure the default upon which such interest is accrued.

21. Expense of Enforcement. If either Lessor or Lessee should prevail in any litigation by or against the other party related to this Lease, or if either party should become a party to any litigation instituted by or against the other with respect to any third party, then as between Lessor and Lessee, the losing party shall indemnify and hold the prevailing party harmless from all costs and reasonable attorney's fees incurred by the prevailing party in connection with such litigation.

22. Inspection. Lessee will permit Lessor, its agents, employees, and contractors to enter all parts of the Premises to inspect the same and to enforce or carry out any provisions of this Lease.

23. Non-Waiver. Lessor's or Lessee's failure to insist upon strict performance of any covenant of this Lease or to exercise any option or right herein contained shall not be a waiver or relinquishment for the future of such covenant, right, or option, but the same shall remain in full force and effect.

24. Captions. The captions and headings herein are for convenience and reference only and should not be used in interpreting any provision of this Lease.

25. Applicable Law. This Lease shall be governed by and construed under the laws of the State of Colorado. If any provision of this Lease, or portion thereof, or the application thereof to any person or circumstance shall,

to any extent, be invalid or unenforceable, the remainder of this Lease shall not be affected thereby, and each provision of this Lease shall be valid and enforceable to the fullest extent permitted by law. Time is of the essence in this Lease.

26. Successors. This Lease and the covenants and conditions herein contained shall inure to the benefit of and be binding upon Lessor, its successors, and assigns; and shall be binding upon Lessee, its heirs, executors, administrators, successors, and assigns; and shall inure to the benefit of Lessee and only such assigns of Lessee to whom the assignment by Lessee has been consented to by Lessor.

27. Force Majeure. The time within which any of the parties hereto shall be required to perform any act or acts under this Lease, including the performance of Lessor's and Lessee's work, shall be extended to the extent that the performance of such act or acts shall be delayed by acts of God, fire, windstorm, flood, explosion, collapse of structures, riot, war, labor disputes, delays, or restrictions by governmental bodies, inability to obtain or use necessary materials, or any cause beyond the reasonable control of such party, other than lack of monies or inability to procure monies to fulfill its commitment or obligation under this Lease; provided, however, that the party entitled to such extension hereunder shall give prompt notice to the other party of the occurrence causing such delay. The provisions of this Item 27 shall not operate to excuse Lessee from prompt payment of rent, additional rent, or any other payments required by the terms of this Lease. Either party may terminate this Lease without penalty if a force majeure event lasts for more than sixty (60) consecutive days.

28. Substitute Space. This section intentionally omitted.

29. Amendments in Writing. This Lease and the Exhibits attached hereto and forming a part hereof set forth all the covenants, promises, agreements, conditions, and understandings between Lessor and Lessee concerning the Premises, and there are no covenants, promises, agreements, conditions, or understandings, oral or written, between them other than are herein set forth. Except as herein otherwise provided, no subsequent alteration, amendment, change, or addition to this Lease

shall be binding upon Lessor and Lessee unless reduced to writing and signed by both parties.

30. Authority. Lessee, if a corporation, warrants and represents to Lessor that Lessee's execution of this Lease has been duly authorized by the Lessee's Board of Directors.

31. Copies. This Lease shall be executed in multiple copies, any one of which may be considered and used as an original.

IN WITNESS WHEREOF, the parties have hereto executed this instrument on the day and year first written above.

Giant Real Estate Company   Tree Services, Inc.

By: _____/s/Jack Money_____   By: _____/s/Melissa Green_____
    Jack Money, President   Melissa Green, CEO &
                                                President

Exhibits A and B

These exhibits were intentionally omitted.

**Revolving Line of Credit and Security Agreement between
Tree Services, Inc. and Big Bank**

Revolving Line of Credit and Security Agreement[2]

This REVOLVING LINE OF CREDIT AND SECURITY AGREEMENT is dated as of June 15, 2008, between Big Bank (the "Bank") and Tree Services, Inc. (the "Borrower").

In order to induce the Bank to advance money or grant other financial accommodations on one or more occasions to the undersigned Borrower, the undersigned Borrower represents, warrants, covenants to and agrees with the Bank as follows:

1. Definitions

For purposes of this Agreement, unless the context clearly requires otherwise, in addition to the terms defined elsewhere herein, the following terms shall have the meanings set forth below:

Affiliate means any person or entity, which directly or indirectly controls, or is controlled by, or is under common control with the Borrower.

Agreement means this Revolving Line of Credit and Security Agreement.

Base Rate means the interest rate announced by the Bank from time to time as its Base Rate.

Collateral means the collateral described in Section 3.1 hereof.

Control shall be deemed to exist if any person, entity or corporation, or combination thereof shall have possession, directly or indirectly, of the power to direct the management or policies of the Borrower or any person, entity, or corporation deemed to be an Affiliate of the Borrower, and shall be deemed to include any holder of 51% or more of any stock or other interest in the Borrower or in any person, entity or corporation deemed to be an Affiliate of the Borrower, whether such holding is direct or indirect.

Events of Default shall have the meaning given such term in Section 8 of this Agreement.

Guarantor means any guarantor, endorser or surety of any obligation of the Borrower to the Bank.

Indebtedness means the total of all obligations of the Borrower to the Bank, whether current or long-term, including without limitation, guaranties, endorsements, or other arrangements whereby responsibility is assumed for the obligations of others.

---

[2] This contract was adapted from *Loan and Security Agreement for Revolving Credit Facility—Master Form with Commentary*, 15 Business Transactions Solutions §75:118 (June 2014).

Legal Requirements means all applicable present and future statutes, laws, ordinances, rules and regulations of any governmental authority, all orders, writs, injunctions, decrees and determinations and all covenants which bind or materially affect the Borrower or any part of its assets.

Line of Credit means the Borrower's Line of Credit with the Bank referred to in Section 2.1 hereof.

Line Note means the Borrower's Promissory Note evidencing indebtedness for the Line of Credit.

Loan Account means the accounting as to the Loans by the Bank pursuant to Section 2.2 hereof.

Loan Documents means the following documents collectively:

(i) This Agreement;

(ii) Each Promissory Note of the Borrower to the Bank, including the Line Note (collectively the "Notes") evidencing the indebtedness for the Loan;

(iii) All other documents and instruments heretofore or hereafter executed by the Borrower, or any Guarantor in favor of the Bank relating to the Loans including any guaranty, pledge, security or subordination agreement and related Uniform Commercial Code financing statements; and

(iv) In each case, the term "Loan Documents" and any reference herein to any particular Loan Document shall mean and include all amendments, modifications, replacements, renewals or extensions of any and all such documents whenever executed.

The Loan Documents in effect as of the date hereof are identified on Schedule 1 hereto.

Loans means:

(i) The Line of Credit evidenced by the Line Note; and

(ii) Any other loans made by the Bank to the Borrower after the date of this Agreement.

Obligations means all liabilities and obligations now or hereafter owing from the Borrower to the Bank of whatever kind or nature, whether or not currently contemplated at the time of this Agreement, whether such obligations be direct or indirect, absolute or contingent or due or to become due, including all obligations of the Borrower, actual or contingent, in respect of letters of credit or banker's acceptances issued by the Bank for the account of or guaranteed by the Borrower, including without limitation all obligations of any partnership or joint venture as to which the Borrower is or may become liable, which term shall include all accrued interest and all costs and expenses, including reasonable attorneys' fees, costs and expenses relating to the appraisal and/or valuation of assets and all reasonable costs and expenses incurred or paid by the Bank in exercising, preserving, defending, collecting, enforcing or protecting any of its rights under the Obligations or in any litigation arising out of the transactions evidenced by the Obligations.

Required Permits means all permits, licenses, approvals, consents and waivers necessary pursuant to any Legal Requirement to be obtained from or made by any governmental authority for the ownership by the Borrower of its assets or for the conduct of its business.

Termination Date shall have the meaning set forth in Section 2.1 hereof.

2. Loans

2.1. Line of Credit

(a) Line of Credit. Pursuant to this Agreement and upon satisfaction of the conditions precedent in Section 5 hereof, during the period from the date hereof until the first anniversary hereof (as such date may be extended in writing from time to time, in the Bank's sole and absolute discretion, the "Termination Date"), the Bank shall make advances under the Line of Credit and the Borrower may borrow, repay and re-borrow under the Line of Credit; provided, however, that the aggregate amount of all advances at any one time outstanding shall not exceed $750,000.

(b) Line of Credit Advances. All advances under the Line of Credit shall be evidenced by the Line Note, shall bear interest and prepayment premiums thereunder and shall be due and payable in full on the Termination Date.

2.2. Loan Account

(a) The Bank shall maintain an accounting (the "Loan Account") on its books to record: (i) all Loans; (ii) all payments made by the Borrower; and (iii) all other appropriate debits and credits as provided in this Agreement with respect to the Obligations. All entries in the Loan Account shall be made in accordance with the Bank's customary accounting practices as in effect from time to time. Borrower irrevocably waives the right to direct the application of any and all payments at any time or times thereafter received by the Bank from or on behalf of Borrower, and the Borrower hereby irrevocably agrees that the Bank shall have the continuing exclusive right to apply and to reapply any and all payments received at any time or times after the occurrence and during the continuance of an Event of Default against the Obligations in such manner as the Bank may deem advisable.

(b) The balance in the Loan Account, as set forth on the Bank's most recent printout or other written statement, shall be presumptive evidence of the amounts due and owing to the Bank by Borrower; provided, however, that any failure to so record or any error in so recording shall not affect the payment of the Obligations. Any periodic statement prepared by the Bank setting forth the principal balance of the Loan Account and the calculation of interest due thereon shall be subject to subsequent adjustment by the Bank but shall, absent manifest errors or omissions, be presumed final, conclusive and binding upon the Borrower, and shall constitute an account stated unless within three (3) days after receipt of such statement, the Borrower shall deliver to the Bank its written objection thereto specifying the error or errors, if any, contained in such statement. In the absence of a written objection delivered to the Bank as set forth above, the Bank's statement of the Loan Account shall be presumptive evidence against the Borrower of the amount of the Obligations and the burden of proof to show manifest errors or omissions shall be on the Borrower.

3. Grant of Security Interest; Obligations Secured

3.1. Grant of Security Interest

The Borrower hereby grants to the Bank a security interest in all of the Borrower's present and future right, title and interest in and to any and all of the following property wherever located and whether now existing or hereafter created or arising (collectively, the "Collateral"):

(a) All equipment, as defined in the Uniform Commercial Code (the "Uniform Commercial Code") and all machinery, tools, parts, and motor vehicles, tangible or intangible, presently owned or hereafter acquired by the Borrower, together with all additions and accessions thereto and substitutions and replacements therefor (herein, collectively "Equipment"), and all products and proceeds (including insurance and condemnation proceeds) thereof;

3.2. Obligations Secured

The security interest in the Collateral granted herein is to secure the payment and performance of the Obligations.

4. Representations and Warranties

The Borrower hereby represents and warrants to the Bank (which representations and warranties will survive the delivery of this Agreement and the making of any advances of any Loan and shall be deemed to be continuing until all Loans are fully paid and this Agreement is terminated) that:

(a) (i) The Borrower is and will continue to be, duly organized and validly existing; the Borrower is in good standing under the laws of the State of Colorado; (ii) the Borrower is qualified and in good standing to do business in all other jurisdictions in which the property owned, leased or operated by it or the nature of the business conducted by it makes such qualification necessary; (iii) the Borrower has the power to execute and deliver this Agreement and each other Loan Document and to borrow hereunder; and (iv) the Borrower has all Required Permits without unusual restrictions or limitations, to own, operate and lease its properties and to conduct the business in which it is presently engaged, all of which are in full force and effect.

(b) The making and performance by the Borrower of this Agreement and the Loan Documents have been authorized by all necessary corporate action by its board of directors. The execution and delivery of this Agreement and the other Loan Documents, the consummation of the transactions herein and therein contemplated, the fulfillment of or compliance with the terms and provisions hereof and thereof, (i) are within its powers, (ii) will not violate any provision of law or of its organizational documents, or (iii) will not result in the breach of, or constitute a default under, or result in the creation of any lien, charge or encumbrance upon any property or assets of the Borrower pursuant to any indenture or bank loan or credit agreement (other than pursuant to this Agreement and the other Loan Documents) or other agreement or instrument to which the Borrower is a party. To the Borrower's knowledge, no approval, authorization, consent or other order or registration or filing with any governmental body is required in connection with the making and performance of this Agreement.

(c) The financial statement(s) attached hereto as Schedule 2, were prepared in conformity with GAAP and are correct and complete and fairly present the financial condition and the results of operations of the Borrower for the periods and as of the dates thereof. The Borrower has no direct or contingent liabilities not disclosed in such statements. Since the date of the latest financial statement in Schedule 2, there has been no material adverse change in the assets, liabilities, financial condition or business of the Borrower.

(d) Subject to any limitations stated therein or in connection therewith, all information furnished or to be furnished by the Borrower pursuant to the terms hereof is, or will be at the time the same is furnished, accurate and complete in all material respects necessary in order to make the information furnished, in the light of the circumstances under which such information is furnished, not misleading.

(e) The Borrower is in material compliance with all Legal Requirements applicable to it, its property or the conduct of its business, including, without limitation, those pertaining to or concerning the employment of labor, employee benefits, public health, safety and the environment.

(f) No proceedings by or before any private, public or governmental body, agency or authority and no litigation is pending, or, so far as is known to the Borrower, or any of Borrower's officers threatened against the Borrower, except such as are disclosed in Schedule 3 attached hereto.

(g) No Event of Default has occurred and no event has occurred or is continuing which, pursuant to the provisions of Section 8, with the lapse of time and/or the giving of a notice specified therein, would constitute such an Event of Default.

(h) The Borrower shall use the proceeds of each advance of each Loan for general commercial purposes related to liquidity, provided that no part of such proceeds will be used, in whole or in part, for the purpose of purchasing or carrying any "margin stock" as such term is defined in

Regulation U of the Board of Governors of the Federal Reserve System.

(i)　This Agreement and all other Loan Documents, upon the execution and delivery thereof, will be legal, valid, binding and enforceable obligations of the Borrower or the person executing the same, as the case may be, in accordance with the terms of each; provided, however, that the Borrower's representation as to enforceability is qualified to the extent that enforcement of the rights and remedies created by this Agreement and the Loan Documents may be subject to applicable bankruptcy, insolvency, reorganization or similar laws affecting the rights of creditors and secured parties generally, and does not apply with respect to the availability of the remedy of specific performance, injunctive relief or any other equitable remedy.

(j)　The Borrower has good and marketable title to its properties and assets, including all of the Collateral, subject to no mortgage, pledge, lien, security interest, encumbrance or other charge which is not set forth in Schedule 4 attached hereto.

(k)　The Borrower has filed all tax returns and reports required to be filed by it with all federal, state or local authorities and has paid in full or made adequate provision for the payment of all taxes, interest, penalties, assessments or deficiencies shown to be due or claimed to be due on or in respect of such tax returns and reports.

(l)　The Borrower conducts its business solely in its own name without the use of a trade name or the intervention of or through any other entity of any kind, other than as disclosed on Schedule 5 attached hereto. All books and records relating to the assets of the Borrower are located at the Borrower's chief executive office and its other places and locations, where its assets are located, all of which are set forth on Schedule 6 attached hereto.

(m)　The Borrower has not given nor received, any notice that: (i) there has been a release, or there is a threat of release, of toxic substances, oil or hazardous wastes on or from any real property owned or operated by the Borrower; (ii) the Borrower may be or is liable for the costs of cleaning up or responding to a release of any toxic substances, oil or hazardous wastes; or (iii) any of such real property is subject to a lien for any liability arising from costs incurred in response to a release of toxic substances, oil or hazardous wastes.

(n) The Borrower and each Affiliate is in compliance in all material respects with all applicable provisions of ERISA, the Internal Revenue Code, and all other applicable laws and the regulations and interpretations thereof with respect to all Employee Benefit Plans, as defined in ERISA. No liability has been incurred by it or any of its Affiliates with respect to any unfunded liability, or for any taxes or penalties with respect to any such Employee Benefit Plan. The term "ERISA" means the Employee Retirement Income Security Act of 1974, as amended from time to time, and any successor statute and all rules and regulations promulgated thereunder.

5. Conditions Precedent

5.1. Conditions to Initial Advance

In addition to any other conditions contained in this Agreement, the initial advance under the Line of Credit shall be subject to the following conditions precedent:

(a) Approval of Bank Counsel. All legal matters incident to the transactions hereby contemplated shall be satisfactory to counsel for the Bank.

(b) Proof of Action. The Bank shall have received such documents evidencing the Borrower's power to execute and deliver this Agreement and the other Loan Documents as the Bank or its counsel shall request.

(c) The Notes and Loan Documents. The Borrower shall have delivered to the Bank the Notes, this Agreement, the other Loan Documents and such other documents as the Bank may request.

(d) Opinion of Counsel. The Bank shall have received from counsel for the Borrower a written opinion, satisfactory in form and substance to the Bank and its counsel.

(e) Liens to be Discharged. The Bank shall be satisfied with arrangements made to pay, discharge and terminate debt owed and security interests granted by the Borrower to non-permitted debt and security interest holders.

5.2. Conditions to Every Advance

In addition to all other conditions contained in this Agreement, every advance under the Line of Credit shall be subject to the following conditions precedent that:

(a) No Event of Default. No Event of Default has occurred and no event shall have occurred or be continuing which, pursuant to the provisions of Section 8, with the lapse of time and/or the giving of a notice as specified therein, would constitute an Event of Default.

(b) No Material Adverse Change. There shall have been no material adverse change (as determined by the Bank in its sole and absolute discretion) in the assets, liabilities, financial condition or business of the Borrower or any Guarantor since the date of any financial statements delivered to the Bank before or after the date of this Agreement.

(c) Representations and Warranties. That the representations and warranties contained in Section 4 hereof and in each other Loan Document shall be true and correct in all material respects. Any request for a borrowing shall be deemed a certification by the Borrower as to the truth and accuracy in all material respects of the representations and warranties contained in Section 4 hereof and in each other Loan Document as of the date of such request.

6. Affirmative Covenants

The Borrower covenants and agrees that from the date hereof until payment in full of all Loans and the performance of all Borrower's obligations hereunder and under all other Loan Documents is complete and this Agreement shall have terminated, unless the Bank otherwise consents in writing, the Borrower shall:

(a) Comply with all terms and conditions of this Agreement and the other Loan Documents and pay all material debts of the Borrower before the same shall become delinquent.

(b) The Borrower shall deliver to the Bank: (i) within twenty (15) days after the close of each quarter, a balance sheet of the Borrower as of the close of each quarter and statements of income and retained earnings for that portion of the fiscal year-to-date then ended, prepared in conformity with GAAP, and certified by the Chief Financial Officer of the Borrower as accurate, true and complete; (ii) within forty-five (45) days after the close of each fiscal year of the Borrower, in final, unaudited, financial statements ("Financial Statements") including, a balance sheet as of the close of such year and statements of income and retained earnings and cash flows for the year then ended, prepared in conformity with GAAP, applied on a basis consistent with that of the preceding year or containing disclosure of the effect on financial position or results of operations of any change in the application of accounting principles during the year and certified by the Chief Financial Officer of the Borrower as accurate, true, and complete; (iii) simultaneously with the delivery of the financial statements required in (ii) above a Certificate of Compliance certifying that, as at the end of the applicable period, the Borrower is in compliance with all covenants set forth in this Agreement and in each other Loan Document and certified by the Chief Financial Officer or independent accountant of the Borrower, as accurate, true and complete; (iv) the other financial reports, if any, delivered to the shareholders of the Borrower, and upon request, such other information about the financial condition, business and operations of the Borrower and each Guarantor, as the Bank may from time to time, reasonably request; and (v) promptly upon becoming aware of any Event of Default, or any event which with the giving of notice or the passage of time would constitute an Event of Default, notice thereof, in writing.

(c)   (i) Keep its properties insured against fire and other hazards (so called "All Risk" coverage) in amounts and with companies satisfactory to the Bank to the same extent and covering such risks as is customary in the same or a similar business, but in no event in an amount less than the full insurable value thereof, which policies shall name the Bank as loss payee as its interest may appear, (ii) maintain public liability coverage against claims for personal injuries or death, and (iii) maintain all workers' compensation, employment or similar insurance as may be required by applicable law. Such All Risk property insurance coverage shall provide for a minimum of ten (10) days' written notice to the Bank of cancellation or modification. The Borrower agrees to deliver copies of all of the aforesaid insurance policies to the Bank. In the event of any loss or damage to any of its assets, including any collateral securing any Loan, the Borrower shall give prompt written notice to the Bank and to Borrower's insurers of such loss or damage and shall promptly file proofs of loss with said insurers.

(d)   Comply with all Legal Requirements, including without limitation, those pertaining to or concerning the employment of labor, employee benefits, public health, safety and the environment. The Borrower shall pay all taxes, assessments, governmental charges or levies, or claims for labor, supplies, rent and other obligations made against the Borrower or any of its properties which, if unpaid, might become a lien or charge against it or any of its properties, except liabilities being contested in good faith with the prior written consent of the Bank and against which, if requested by the Bank, the Borrower shall maintain reserves in amount and in form (book, cash, bond or otherwise) satisfactory to the Bank.

(e) Maintain its chief executive office, principal places of business and locations of assets at the locations set forth in this Agreement. The Borrower shall promptly give the Bank written notice of any change in any of such addresses. All business records of the Borrower, including those pertaining to all Accounts and contract rights, shall be kept at the said chief executive office of the Borrower, unless prior written consent of the Bank is obtained to a change of location.

(f) Allow the Bank by or through any of its officers, agents, attorneys, or accountants designated by it, for the purpose of ascertaining whether or not each and every provision hereof and of any other Loan Document is being performed and for the purpose of examining and appraising the assets of the Borrower and the auditing records relating thereto, to enter the offices of the Borrower to examine or inspect any of the properties, books and records or extracts therefrom and to make copies thereof and to discuss the affairs, finances and accounts thereof with the Borrower and its accountants as often as the Bank may determine. The Borrower will reimburse the Bank for all costs associated with its examination, appraisals and audits.

(g) Within five (5) business days advise the Bank of the commencement of or threat of litigation, including arbitration proceedings and any proceedings before any governmental agency, which might have a material adverse effect upon the assets, liabilities, financial condition or business of the Borrower.

(h) Within five (5) business days notify the Bank in writing of (i) any enforcement, cleanup, removal or other action instituted or threatened against the Borrower or any Guarantors by any federal, state, county or municipal authority or agency pursuant to any public health, safety or environmental laws, rules, ordinances and regulations, (ii) any and all claims made or threatened by any third party against the Borrower or any Guarantor or any real property owned or operated by any of them relating to the existence of, or damage, loss or injury from any toxic substances, oil or hazardous wastes or any other conditions constituting actual or potential violations of such laws, rules, ordinances or regulations, and (iii) any enforcement or compliance action, instituted or threatened or claim made or threatened by any federal or state authority relating to the employment of labor or employee benefits.

(i)   Continue to conduct the business of the Borrower as presently conducted, maintain its existence and maintain its properties in good repair, working order and operating condition. The Borrower shall promptly notify the Bank of any event causing material loss or unusual depreciation in the value of the business assets of the Borrower and the amount of same.

(j)   The Borrower will notify the Bank promptly upon Borrower's entry into any transaction with any federal, state or local governmental entity which would give rise to an account receivable which would be subject to the Federal Assignment of Claims Act, or any other comparable federal, state or local legal requirement (herein a "Government Account") and the Borrower will execute all such instruments and take all such action as may be reasonably requested by the Bank so that all moneys due or to become due thereunder will be effectively assigned to the Bank and notice thereof given to such account debtor in accordance with the Federal Assignment of Claims Act, or any other comparable federal, state or local legal requirement.

(k)   (i) The Borrower will keep the Collateral in good order and repair, will not waste or destroy the Collateral or any part thereof and will not knowingly use the Collateral in violation of any applicable Legal Requirement or any policy of insurance thereon. The Borrower will notify the Bank in writing promptly upon its learning of any event, condition, loss, damage, litigation, administrative proceeding or other circumstance which may materially and adversely affect the assets, liabilities, financial condition or business of the Borrower or the Bank's security interest in the Collateral. In the event that the Bank shall reasonably determine that there has been any loss, damage or material diminution in the value of the Collateral, the Borrower will, whenever the Bank requests, pay to the Bank such amount as the Bank shall have reasonably determined represents such loss, damage or material diminution in value (any such payment not to affect the Bank's security interest in such Collateral). (ii) Without limiting the generality of the foregoing, the Borrower shall notify the Bank promptly of any claim or dispute that may materially affect the value of the Borrower's Collateral.

(l) The Borrower will at such intervals as the Bank may request, notify the Bank, upon a form satisfactory to the Bank, of all Collateral which has come into existence since the date hereof or the date of the last such notification.

(m) At its option, but without obligation to do so, the Bank may discharge taxes, liens, security interests or other encumbrances at any time levied or placed on the Collateral; may place and pay for insurance on the Collateral; may order and pay for the repair, maintenance and preservation of the Collateral; and may pay any fees for filing or recording such instruments or documents as may be necessary or desirable to perfect the security interest granted herein. The Borrower agrees to reimburse the Bank on demand for any payment made or any expense incurred by the Bank pursuant to the foregoing authorization, and all such payments and expenses shall constitute part of the principal amount of Obligations hereby secured and shall bear interest at the highest rate payable on the Obligations of the Borrower to the Bank.

(n) The Borrower shall use the Bank for all of the Borrower's commercial banking needs. The Bank is hereby authorized but not obligated to charge any of the Borrower's accounts with the Bank to pay any of the Borrower's Obligations.

7. Negative Covenants

The Borrower covenants and agrees that until payment is made in full of all Loans, the performance of all Borrower's obligations hereunder and under all other Loan Documents is complete and this Agreement shall have terminated, unless the Bank otherwise consents in writing in its sole and absolute discretion, the Borrower shall not:

(a) Incur or permit to exist any lien, mortgage, security interest, pledge, charge or other encumbrance against any of its property or assets, whether now owned or hereafter acquired (including, without limitation, any lien or encumbrance relating to any response, removal or cleanup of any toxic substances, oil or hazardous wastes), except: (i) liens in favor of the Bank required by this Agreement or any other Loan Document; (ii) pledges or deposits in connection with or to secure workers' compensation and unemployment insurance; (iii) tax liens which are being contested in good faith; and (iv) liens, mortgages, security interests, pledges, charges or other encumbrances in favor of the Bank or specifically permitted, in writing, by the Bank.

(b) Create or incur any Indebtedness for borrowed money, become liable, either actually or contingently, in respect of letters of credit or banker's acceptances or issue or sell any obligations of the Borrower, excluding, however, from the operation of this covenant the Loans hereunder and all other Obligations of the Borrower to the Bank.

(c) Sell, lease, pledge, transfer or otherwise dispose of all or any of its assets (other than the disposition of inventory in the ordinary course of its business as presently conducted or the sale of obsolete equipment or equipment no longer usable in the conduct of the Borrower's business), whether now owned or hereafter acquired except for liens or encumbrances required or permitted hereby or by any Loan Document.

(d) Assume, guarantee, endorse or otherwise become liable upon the obligations of any person, firm or corporation or by the endorsement of negotiable instruments for deposit or collection or similar transactions in the ordinary course of business.

(e) Change its name or conduct its business under any trade name or style other than as hereinabove set forth or change its chief executive office, places of business or the present locations of its assets of records relating thereto from those addresses set forth on Schedule 7 attached hereto.

(f) Except as otherwise permitted herein, acquire, form or dispose of any Affiliate or acquire all or substantially all or any material portion of the stock or assets of any other person, firm or corporation.

(g) Make or consent to a material change in the ownership or capital structure of the Borrower, or make a material change in the management of the Borrower or in the manner in which the business of the Borrower is conducted or in its method of accounting.

(h) Allow any business or activity to be conducted on real property owned or occupied by the Borrower that uses, manufactures, treats, stores or disposes of any toxic substances, oil or hazardous wastes which are prohibited or regulated pursuant to any Legal Requirement, except in full compliance therewith and with all Required Permits, or which are contrary to the provisions of any insurance policy.

8. Events of Default; Remedies

8.1. Events of Default

The occurrence of any of the following events, for any reason whatsoever, shall constitute an "Event of Default" hereunder:

(a) (i) Failure to make due payment of principal or interest on any Loan provided such failure continues for a period of three (3) business days or (ii) failure by the Borrower, any Affiliate, or any Guarantor to make due payment of any other liability or obligation owing by the Borrower, any Affiliate or any Guarantor to the Bank, now existing or hereafter incurred, whether direct or contingent (herein, "Other Bank Debt"), provided such failure continues for a period of three (3) business days; or

(b) Failure by the Borrower or any Guarantor to observe or perform any covenant contained in (i) this Agreement, or any of their respective obligations under any other Loan Document or (ii) any document or instrument evidencing, securing or otherwise relating to any Other Bank Debt provided that if said failure is curable, it continues for a period of ten (10) days; or

(c) Any representation or warranty made by the Borrower or any Guarantor to the Bank or any statement, certificate or other data furnished by any of them in connection herewith or with any other Loan Document proves at any time to be incorrect in any material respect; or

(d) A judgment or judgments for the payment of money shall be rendered against the Borrower or any Guarantor which shall remain unsatisfied and in effect for a period of ten (10) days without a stay of execution; or

(e) Any levy, seizure, attachment, execution or similar process shall be issued or levied on any of the Borrower's or any Guarantor's property, which such process could have a material adverse effect on the business of the Borrower in the Bank's reasonable judgment; or

(f) The Borrower or any Guarantor shall (i) apply for or consent to the appointment of a receiver, conservator, trustee or liquidator of all or a substantial part of any of its assets; (ii) be unable, or admit in writing its inability, to pay its debts as they mature; (iii) file or permit the filing of any petition, case, arrangement, reorganization, or the like under any insolvency or bankruptcy law, or the adjudication of it as a bankrupt, or the making of an assignment for the benefit of creditors or the consenting to any form of arrangement for the satisfaction, settlement or delay of debt or the appointment of a receiver for all or any part of its properties; or (iv) take any action for the purpose of effecting any of the foregoing; or

(g) An order, judgment or decree shall be entered, or a case shall be commenced, against the Borrower or any Guarantor, without the application, approval or consent of the Borrower or such Guarantor by or in any court of competent jurisdiction, approving a petition or permitting the commencement of a case seeking reorganization or liquidation of the Borrower or any Guarantor or appointing a receiver, trustee, conservator or liquidator of the Borrower or any Guarantor, or of all or a substantial part of its assets and the Borrower or any Guarantor, by any act, indicates its approval thereof, consent thereto, or acquiescence therein, or, in any event, such order, judgment, decree or case shall continue unstayed, or undismissed and in effect for any period of ninety (90) consecutive days; or

(h) All Guarantors who are natural persons shall die; or

(i) The Borrower or any Guarantor shall dissolve or liquidate, or be dissolved or liquidated, or cease to exist legally, or merge or consolidate with, or be merged or consolidated with or into any other entity; or

(j) Failure by the Borrower or by any Guarantor to pay or perform any other Obligation whether contingent or otherwise, or if any such other Obligation shall be accelerated, or if there exists any event of default under any instrument, document or agreement governing, evidencing or securing such other Obligation; or

(k) The Bank believes in its sole and absolute discretion that any material adverse change in the assets, liabilities, financial condition or business of the Borrower or any Guarantor has occurred since the date of any financial statements delivered to the Bank before or after the date of this Agreement; or

(l) The Borrower sells, liquidates, transfers or otherwise disposes of an asset not in strict accordance with the terms of this Loan Agreement; or

(m) If at any time the Bank reasonably believes in good faith that the prospect of payment of any Obligation or the performance of any agreement of the Borrower or any Guarantor is materially impaired, or that there is such a change in the assets, liabilities, financial condition or business of the Borrower or any Guarantor as the Bank believes in good faith materially impairs the Bank's security or increases its risk of non-collection.

8.2. Remedies

(a) Upon the occurrence of any Event of Default and at any time thereafter, the availability of advances hereunder and under the Line of Credit shall, at the option of the Bank, be deemed to be automatically terminated and the Bank, at its option, may declare one or more or all of the Loans outstanding hereunder, together with accrued interest thereon and all applicable late charges and surcharges and all other liabilities and obligations of the Borrower to the Bank to be forthwith due and payable, whereupon the same shall become forthwith due and payable; all of the foregoing without presentment or demand for payment, notice of non-payment, protest or any other notice or demand of any kind, all of which are expressly waived by the Borrower and by each Guarantor.

(b) The Bank shall have the following additional rights and remedies:

(i) All of the rights and remedies of a secured party under the Uniform Commercial Code or any other applicable law or at equity, all of which rights and remedies shall be cumulative and non-exclusive, to the extent permitted by law, in addition to any other rights and remedies contained in this Agreement, any other Loan Document or in any document, instrument or agreement evidencing, governing or securing the Obligations.

(ii) The right to (1) take possession of the Collateral, without resort to legal process and without prior notice to Borrower, and for that purpose Borrower hereby irrevocably appoints the Bank its attorney-in-fact to enter upon any premises on which the Collateral or any part thereof may be situated and remove the Collateral therefrom, or (2) require the Borrower to assemble the Collateral and make it available to the Bank in a place to be designated by the Bank, in its sole discretion. The Borrower shall make available to the Bank all premises, locations and facilities necessary for the Bank's taking possession of the Collateral or for removing or putting the Collateral in saleable form.

(iii) The right to sell or otherwise dispose of all or any part of the Collateral by one or more public or private sales. Unless the Collateral is perishable or threatens to decline speedily in value or is of a type customarily sold on a recognized market, the Bank will give the Borrower at least five (5) business days' prior written notice of the time and place of any public sale thereof or of the time after which any private sale or any other intended disposition (which may include, without limitation, a public sale or lease of all or part of the Collateral) is to be made. The Borrower agrees that five (5) business days is a reasonable time for any such notice. The Bank, its employees, attorneys and agents may bid and become purchasers at any such sale, if public, and may purchase at any private sale any of the Collateral that is of a type customarily sold on a recognized market or which is subject to widely distributed standard price quotations. Any public or private sale shall be free from any right of redemption, which the Borrower hereby waives and releases. If there is a deficiency after such sale and the application of the net proceeds from such sale, the Borrower shall be responsible for the same, with interest.

(iv) The right, after an Event of Default shall have occurred (and Borrower irrevocably appoints the Bank as attorney-in-fact for the Borrower for this purpose, such appointment being coupled with an interest), upon notice to Borrower and without resort to legal process, to notify the persons liable for payment of all accounts (as defined in the Uniform Commercial Code) at any time and direct such persons to make payments directly to the Bank, and to perform all acts the Borrower could take to collect on such accounts, including, without limitation, the right to notify postal authorities to change the address for delivery, open mail, endorse checks, bring collection suits, and realize upon Collateral securing such accounts. At the Bank's request, all bills and statements sent by the Borrower to the persons liable for payments of such accounts shall state that they have been assigned to, and are solely payable to, the Bank, and Borrower shall direct persons liable for the payment of such accounts to pay directly to the Bank any sums due or to become due on account thereof.

(v) The right from and after an Event of Default, from time to time without demand or notice, and without being required to look first to any other Collateral to apply and set off any or all of the Deposits and Securities against, any and all Obligations even though such Obligations be unmatured.

9. Lien and Set Off

The Borrower and each Guarantor hereby give the Bank a lien and right of set off for all of Borrower's and each Guarantor's liabilities and obligations to the Bank upon and against all the deposits, credits, Collateral and property of the Borrower and each Guarantor now or hereafter in the possession, custody, safekeeping or control of the Bank or in transit to it.

10. Miscellaneous

10.1. Joint and Several Obligations; Certain Waivers

(a) This Agreement shall be the joint and several obligation of the Borrower and each Guarantor and each provision of this Agreement shall apply to each and all jointly and severally and to the property and liabilities of each and all, all of whom hereby waive diligence, demand, presentment for payment, notice of nonpayment, protest and notice of dishonor, and who hereby agree to any extension or delay in the time for payment or enforcement, to renewal of any Loan and to any substitution or release of any Collateral or any Guarantor, all without notice and without any effect on their liabilities. Any delay on the part of the Bank in exercising any right hereunder or under any other Loan Document which may secure any Loan shall not operate as a waiver of any such right, and any waiver granted for one occasion shall not operate as a waiver in the event of a subsequent default. The Bank may revoke any permission or waiver previously granted to Borrower or any Guarantor, such revocation to be effective prospectively when given whether given orally or in writing. The rights and remedies of the Bank shall be cumulative and not in the alternative, and shall include all rights and remedies granted herein, in any other Loan Document and under all applicable laws.

(b) THE BANK, THE BORROWER AND EACH GUARANTOR IRREVOCABLY WAIVE ALL RIGHT TO A TRIAL BY JURY IN ANY PROCEEDING HEREAFTER INSTITUTED BY OR AGAINST THE BANK, THE BORROWER OR ANY GUARANTOR IN RESPECT OF THIS AGREEMENT, THE NOTES OR ANY OTHER LOAN DOCUMENT.

(c) THE BORROWER AND EACH GUARANTOR (i) ACKNOWLEDGE THAT THE TRANSACTION OF WHICH THIS AGREEMENT IS A PART IS A COMMERCIAL TRANSACTION AND (ii) TO THE EXTENT PERMITTED BY ANY STATE OR FEDERAL LAW, WAIVE THE RIGHT ANY OF THEM MAY HAVE TO PRIOR NOTICE OF AND A HEARING ON THE RIGHT OF ANY HOLDER OF THE NOTES, OR ANY OF THEM, TO ANY REMEDY OR COMBINATION OF REMEDIES THAT ENABLES SAID HOLDER, BY WAY OF ATTACHMENT, FOREIGN ATTACHMENT, GARNISHMENT OR REPLEVIN, TO DEPRIVE THE BORROWER OR ANY GUARANTOR OF ANY OF THEIR PROPERTY, AT ANY TIME, PRIOR TO FINAL JUDGMENT IN ANY LITIGATION INSTITUTED IN CONNECTION WITH THIS AGREEMENT.

10.2. Notices

All notices, requests or demands to or upon a party to this Agreement shall be given or made by the other party hereto in writing, in person or by depositing in the mails postage prepaid, return receipt requested addressed to the addressee at the address set forth herein as the Borrower's chief executive office or to such other addresses as such addressee may have designated in writing to the other party hereto. No other method of giving any notice, request or demand is hereby precluded.

10.3. Expenses; Additional Documents

The Borrower will pay all taxes levied or assessed upon the principal sum of the advances made against the Bank and all other fees provided herein, and all expenses arising out of the preparation, amendment, waiver, modification, protection, collection and/or other enforcement of this Agreement, or any other Loan Document, or of any Collateral or security interest now or hereafter granted to secure the Loans or mortgage, security interest or lien granted hereunder or under any other Loan Document (including, without limitation, attorneys' fees). The Borrower will, from time to time, at its expense, execute and deliver to the Bank all such other and further instruments and documents and take or cause to be taken all such other and future action as the Bank shall request in order to effect and confirm or vest more securely all rights contemplated by this Agreement or any other Loan Document.

10.4. Schedules

The Schedules, which are attached hereto, are and shall constitute a part of this Agreement.

10.5. Governing Law; Consent to Jurisdiction

This Agreement, the other Loan Documents and the rights and obligations of the parties hereunder and thereunder shall be construed and interpreted in accordance with the laws of Colorado. The Borrower and each Guarantor agree that the execution of this Agreement and the other Loan Documents and the performance of the Borrower's and Guarantor's obligations hereunder and thereunder shall be deemed to have a Colorado situs and the Borrower and each Guarantor shall be subject to the personal jurisdiction of the courts of Colorado with respect to any action the Bank or its successors or assigns may commence hereunder or thereunder. Accordingly, the Borrower and each Guarantor hereby specifically and irrevocably consent to the jurisdiction of the courts of Colorado with respect to all matters concerning this Agreement, the other Loan Documents, the Notes or the enforcement of any of the foregoing.

10.6. Survival of Representations

All representations, warranties, covenants and agreements herein contained or made in writing in connection with this Agreement shall survive the execution and delivery of the Loan Documents and shall continue in full force and effect until all amounts payable on account of all Loans, the Loan Documents and this Agreement shall have been paid in full and this Agreement has been terminated.

10.7. Integration; Severability; Successors

This Agreement is the final, complete and exclusive statement of the terms governing this Agreement. If any provision of this Agreement shall to any extent be held invalid or unenforceable, then only such provision shall be deemed ineffective and the remainder of this Agreement shall not be affected. The provisions of this Agreement shall bind the heirs, executors, administrators, assigns and successors of the Borrower and each Guarantor and shall inure to the benefit of the Bank, its successors and assigns.

10.8. Determinations as to Compliance

All documents and assurances of any type related to the fulfillment of any condition or compliance with any provision hereof or of any other Loan Document and all other matters related to the Loans are subject to the prior approval and satisfaction of the Bank, its counsel and other consultants.

10.9. Termination of this Agreement

This Agreement shall terminate upon the written agreement of the parties hereto to the termination of any privilege of the Borrower to take advances under the Line of Credit and full and final payment of all amounts with respect to all Loans or otherwise due hereunder and under the other Loan Documents.

IN WITNESS WHEREOF, the undersigned executes this Agreement as an instrument under seal as of the date first set forth above.

Tree Services, Inc.

By: _____/s/Melissa Green_____
         Melissa Green
         CEO & President

ACCEPTED AND AGREED:

Big Bank

By: _____/s/Jack Money_____
         Jack Money, President

Schedules 1–7

All schedules were intentionally omitted.

Website Development and Maintenance Agreement Between Tree Services, Inc. and Webmasters Limited

WEBSITE DEVELOPMENT AND MAINTENANCE AGREEMENT[3]

This Agreement is entered into on June 1, 2014, (the "Effective Date") by and between Tree Services, Inc., a Colorado corporation located at 6789 120th Street, Commerce City, CO 80022 ("Owner") and Webmasters Limited, a Colorado limited liability company located at 1911 S. Broadway, Denver, CO 80202 ("Developer"). Owner and Developer are sometimes referred to collectively in this Agreement as the "Parties."

Owner desires to engage Developer for the following purpose: To develop, create, test, and deliver electronic documents implemented in Hypertext Markup Language ("HTML"), version 4.0 or later, for the purpose of establishing a site for Owner on the World Wide Web (the "Website") and to maintain such Website.

To carry out these purposes, the Parties agree to the following:

1. Definitions

1.1. <u>Browser</u>. The term "Browser" refers to a program used to provide interactive, graphic access to sites on the World Wide Web.

1.2. <u>Excluded Material</u>. See Paragraph 5.5 of this Agreement.

1.3. <u>Internet</u>. The term "Internet" refers to the global network of computers using the TCP/IP protocol for communication.

1.4. <u>Owner's Material</u>. See Paragraph 2.1 of this Agreement.

1.5. <u>Web</u>. The term "Web" refers to the World Wide Web. The Web is a graphic interface used to access sites on the Internet.

1.6. <u>Website Material</u>. See Paragraph 5.1 of this Agreement.

2. Development of Website

2.1. Material to Be Supplied By Owner. Owner will supply to Developer all text, graphics, and other content to be included in the Website ("Owner's Material"). Textual material may be supplied in hard copy or electronic format such as a Word, WordPerfect, or PDF file. Graphic material may be provided in any of the following formats: GIF, PNG, or JPG. Owner's Material may be delivered to Developer by any of the following means: flash drive, e-mail attachment, or File Transfer Protocol ("FTP").

2.2. Developer's Adaptation of Material. Developer will translate and adapt Owner's Material into HTML format, version 4.0 or later, to

---

[3]   This contract was adapted from *Website Development Agreement*, 2 Cal. Transactions Forms—Bus. Transactions § 8:45.

substantially conform to the "mock-up" Web pages attached as Exhibit A.

2.3. Use of Hidden Text. Without prior written permission from Owner, Developer will not include any hidden or invisible text, commands, code, programming, or other material in the Website. Hidden text used for purposes of Web indexing (such as meta tags) will contain the following keywords: landscape, landscaping, landscape services, landscaping services, tree, tree services, tree maintenance, tree removal, tree care, snow removal, and other similar keywords or phrases.

2.4. Access to Site During Construction. During development of the Website, Developer will make the site available for review by Owner at: http://www.tsi.com. Developer will assign a password to the site to prevent unauthorized persons from reviewing its contents. Developer will provide Owner with the password. Developer will not disclose the password to any other person unless directed to do so in writing by Owner. Developer will periodically monitor access to the Website during development and promptly notify Owner if it appears there has been unauthorized access. Developer will not remove the password from the Website until directed to do so in writing by Owner.

2.5. Schedule for Completion Of Website. Development of the Website will proceed according to the milestones set forth in Exhibit B.

2.6. Delivery of Website. Within seven (7) days of completion of the final milestone in Exhibit B, Developer will deliver the Website in both printed and electronic format to Owner. The electronic version of the Website will be delivered on a flash drive or via e-mail or FTP, at Owner's sole option. At the time of delivery, Developer will provide Owner with a list of all hypertext links included in the Website along with a written confirmation that the links have been confirmed as current and accurate.

2.7. Final Acceptance. Within thirty (30) days of receipt of the printed and electronic versions of the Website, Owner will notify Developer of any changes required to bring the Website into conformance with the specifications set forth in Exhibit A. Developer will have fifteen (15) days from the date of notification of the changes to implement the changes. Within ten (10) days of receipt of the revised Website, Owner will notify Developer of any problems with the changes. Developer will have seven (7) days from the date of notification of the problems to correct the problems. This process will continue in seven (7) day intervals until Owner gives written notification to Developer of final acceptance of the Website or the Agreement is terminated.

2.8. Retention Of Backup Copy. Developer will maintain a backup copy of the entire Website for a period of three (3) years from the date of final acceptance of the Website by Owner. At the expiration of the three (3) years or upon termination of this Agreement prior to final approval, Developer will destroy all of its copies of the Website, including electronic and printed formats and all backup copies.

3. Compensation

3.1. Total Price. The total price for all work done in connection with this Agreement is $28,500. The Total Price will be paid in installments as set forth in Exhibit B. As each installment becomes due, Developer will submit an invoice to Owner. Invoices will be paid within ten (10) days of receipt. In the event of a dispute regarding whether a milestone was reached and whether a payment became due, Owner will not be under an obligation to pay the amount purportedly due until the dispute is resolved.

3.2. Termination Before Final Acceptance. If this Agreement is terminated before final acceptance of the Website, Developer will be paid for all work completed up to the date of termination that conforms to the specifications in Exhibit A. Developer must deliver all completed work to Developer within five (5) business days of receipt of payment from Owner.

4. Publicity

4.1. Site Publicity. Within ten (10) days of the date of final completion of the Website, Developer will provide Owner with a list and description of at least forty (40) Internet search engines and directories that may be appropriate for the Website. Owner, in Owner's sole discretion, may select any or all of the search engines and directories identified by Developer for submission of the Website. Developer will submit the Website to the search engines and directories selected by Owner within seven (7) days of receipt of the selection list.

4.2. Developer Credit. For a period of two (2) years from the date of final acceptance of the Website, Owner will include an "acknowledgments" page on the Website. The acknowledgments page will credit Developer as the developer of the Website and provide a link to Developer's home page on the Web. Owner will have full discretion as to the format and placement of the credit. Developer will be responsible for providing Owner with information for the credit and for updating that information as reasonably needed. Including a credit for Developer on the Website does not confer on Developer any copyright, trademark, or other proprietary interest or right in the Website or any portion of it.

5. Ownership of Website and Rights

5.1. Work Made for Hire. The term "Website Material" includes, but is not limited to, all text, graphics, video, audio, programming, code, algorithms, scripts, and applets constituting the Website. Developer agrees and understands that its creation and authorship of the Website Material constitutes a work made for hire, as that term is defined in Section 101 of Title 17 of the United States Code (the Copyright Act).

5.2. Assignment of Copyrights. If all or part of the Website Material is, for any reason, deemed not to be a work made for hire, Developer agrees to execute all documents necessary to transfer to Owner the ownership of any and all rights, including but not limited to copyrights, that Developer may have in the Website Material.

5.3. Waiver of Moral Rights. To the extent that Developer has any moral rights (droit moral) or similar rights in the Website Material under the law of any jurisdiction, Developer expressly waives those rights. Except as provided in Paragraph 4.2 of this Agreement, Developer waives any right to have the Website Material attributed to Developer or to prevent the Website Material from being modified, edited, transformed, or otherwise adapted as Owner may deem necessary.

5.4. Ownership of Website Material. Except for the material specifically identified in Paragraph 5.5 of this Agreement, Owner will own the exclusive rights to and in the Website Material, including, but not limited to, all United States and International copyrights and other intellectual property rights. In the event that this Agreement is terminated before final acceptance, Owner will own the exclusive rights including, but not limited to, all United States and International copyrights and other intellectual property rights, in the portion of the Website Material actually completed.

5.5. Excluded Material. If Developer is unable to grant or assign to Owner the exclusive rights to any portion of the Website Material, that portion of the Website Material will be referred to as "Excluded Material." Developer shall specifically identify all Excluded Material on Exhibit C to this Agreement. Developer's identification will include, at minimum, the following information: (1) the nature of the Excluded Material; (2) the owner of the Excluded Material; (3) Developer's authority to include the Excluded Material in the Website; (4) any restrictions or royalty terms applicable to the use of the Excluded Material in the Website. The only Excluded Material that may be included in the Website is the material specifically identified in Exhibit C. No other Excluded Material can be used in the Website provided that Developer has secured Owner's prior written consent to use the Excluded Material.

5.6. License to Use Excluded Material. Developer will obtain at Developer's own expense an irrevocable, nonexclusive, worldwide, perpetual, royalty-free license for Owner, and Owner's agents and assigns, to exploit the Excluded Material identified in Exhibit C for, among other things, the right to reproduce the Excluded Material, to distribute the Excluded Material, to create derivative materials based on the Excluded Material, to publicly display the Excluded Material, to publicly perform the Excluded Material, and to transmit the Excluded Material digitally or by any other means.

6. Warranties

6.1. Ownership Rights. With the exception of Owner's Material and Excluded Material, Developer represents and warrants as follows:

a.   That Developer is the sole author/creator of all of the Website Material or has obtained all necessary licensing rights for the Website Material;

b.   That Developer has authority to grant, assign, and license the Website Material to Owner;

c.   That the Website Material is not subject to any liens or other security interests; and

d.   That the Website Material does not infringe the copyrights, trademarks, or any other intellectual property or proprietary rights of any third person.

6.2. Quality And Performance Of Website. Developer represents and warrants as follows:

a.   That the Website will be developed in a workmanlike, professional manner;

b.   That the Website will conform to the specifications set forth in Exhibit A; and

c.   That the Website will perform properly when browsed with the latest and most recent previous versions of the following browsers: Internet Explorer, Firefox, Safari, Google Chrome, and other similar browsers.

6.3. Compliance With Applicable Laws. Developer represents and warrants that Developer has complied with all applicable local, state, and federal laws in carrying out its obligations under this Agreement.

7. Indemnity

7. Indemnity. With the exception of the Excluded Material, Owner agrees to indemnify and hold Developer harmless from the claims of any third party relating to the Website Material, including, but not limited to, claims of copyright infringement, violation of trade secrets, invasion of privacy, defamation, and right of publicity.

8. Maintenance

Section 8.1 Maintenance Period. Subject to the terms and conditions of this Agreement, Developer will provide such maintenance services to Owner (the "Maintenance Services") as may be required to maintain and update Owner's Website and the individual components thereof. The initial one-year Maintenance Services period (the "Initial Maintenance Period") shall begin on the date of Final Acceptance pursuant to Section 2.7 and each additional one-year maintenance period thereafter shall begin on the date immediately following the date on which the preceding maintenance period ends (each such period a "Paid Maintenance Period" and together with the Initial Maintenance Period, the "Maintenance Period"). The Maintenance Services shall be of the same scope and character as are generally provided by Developer to all its best maintenance customers.

Section 8.2 Maintenance Fees. During the Initial Maintenance Period, Developer shall perform Maintenance Services at no cost to Owner unless Owner terminates this Agreement. After the Initial Maintenance Period, Owner agrees to subscribe, on an annual basis, for continuing Maintenance Services at Developer's then-current standard annual maintenance fee rates (the "Maintenance Fee"). Owner's annual Maintenance Fee for the one year period immediately following the end of the Initial Maintenance Period shall be fixed $2,160, with the first monthly installment of $180 due on the first anniversary of the date of Final Acceptance. All Maintenance Fees shall be payable on a monthly basis in advance.

9. Confidentiality

9.1. Confidential Information Defined. For purposes of this Agreement, "Confidential Information" includes, but is not limited to, business plans, marketing plans, advertising material, customer lists, business records, projections, product information, financial information, and any other information designated as confidential in writing by Owner.

9.2. Nonconfidential Information. Information is not confidential if it is generally available or known within the Internet industry, it is in the public domain, it was known to Developer before this Agreement was entered into, it was independently received by Developer from a third party, or it was developed independently by Developer.

10. Developer's Obligation of Nondisclosure

10. Developer's Obligation of Nondisclosure. Developer promises and agrees:

    a.   To hold the Confidential Information in strict confidence;

b.   To use the Confidential Information only for purposes of carrying out Developer's obligations under this Agreement;

c.   To only disclose the Confidential Information to those of Developer's officers, employees, agents, and other third parties as are necessary to carry out the purpose of this Agreement; and

d.   Not to disclose the Confidential Information to unnecessary third parties.

11. Miscellaneous Provisions

11.1. Term Of Agreement. This Agreement will take effect on the Effective Date and remain in effect until terminated by one of the Parties.

11.2. Termination. If at any time Owner becomes dissatisfied with Developer's performance of its obligations under this Agreement, Owner may immediately terminate this Agreement by providing one hundred twenty (120) days written notice to Developer. Developer may not terminate this Agreement without the prior written consent of Owner, except in the event that Owner has an installment payment or monthly maintenance payment that is more than thirty (30) days past due.

11.3. No Assignment Of Obligations. Neither Party may assign any of its respective obligations under this Agreement without the express written consent of the other Party except that Developer may utilize outside persons and third party contractors to perform its work where Developer deems necessary without Owner's permission.

11.4. Assignment Of Agreement. If either party attempts to assign this Agreement, this Agreement shall be deemed terminated immediately. Owner shall immediately pay all amounts due under the Agreement to Developer and upon such payment Developer shall deliver all materials developed to the Owner.

11.5. Modifications. This Agreement may be amended at any time and from time to time, but any amendment must be in writing and signed by each Party to be bound.

11.6. Undefined Terms. Terms that are not specifically defined in this Agreement are used as set forth in the California Uniform Commercial Code.

11.7. Joint Drafting And Neutral Construction. This Agreement is a negotiated document and shall be deemed to have been drafted jointly by the Parties, and no rule of construction or interpretation shall apply against any particular Party based on a contention that the Agreement was drafted by one of the Parties. This Agreement shall be construed and interpreted in a neutral manner.

11.8. Validity Of Agreement. If any term, provision, covenant, or condition of this Agreement is held by a court of competent jurisdiction to be invalid or unenforceable, the rest of the Agreement shall remain in full force and effect and shall in no way be affected or invalidated.

11.9. Time Of The Essence. The Parties understand that time is of the essence in carrying out their respective obligations under this Agreement.

11.10. Entire Agreement. This Agreement, including all Exhibits, Appendices, and Attachments, contains the entire agreement of the Parties relating to the rights granted and obligations assumed in this Agreement. Any oral representations or modifications concerning this instrument shall be of no force or effect unless contained in a subsequent written modification signed by the Party to be charged.

11.11. Venue and Applicable Law. This Agreement shall be governed, construed, and interpreted in accordance with the laws of the State of Colorado (without respect to principles of conflicts of law), and the Parties submit to the jurisdiction of and venue in the State of Colorado in any legal proceeding necessary to interpret or enforce this Agreement or any part of this Agreement. OWNER IRREVOCABLY WAIVES ANY AND ALL RIGHT TO TRAIL BY JURY IN ANY LEGAL PROCEEDING ARISING OUT OF OR RELATING TO THIS AGREEMENT OR THE TRANSACTIONS CONTEMPLATED THEREBY.

11.12. Attorney Fees And Costs. In any action brought under this Agreement, the prevailing party shall be entitled to recover its actual costs and attorney's fees and all other litigation costs, including expert witness fees, and all actual attorney's fees and litigation costs incurred in connection with the enforcement of a judgment arising from such action or proceeding. The provisions of the preceding sentence shall be severable from the provisions of this Agreement and shall survive the entry of any such judgment. The Parties submit to jurisdiction and venue in the State of Colorado in any legal proceeding arising regarding this Agreement.

Webmasters Limited

By: ___/s/John Dixon___ Date: June 16, 2014
       President

Tree Services, Inc.

By: ___/s/Thomas Shrub___ Date: June 16, 2014
       President

Exhibits A–C

These exhibits were intentionally omitted.

**Executive Employment Agreement Between
Tree Services, Inc. and Melissa Green**

Executive Employment Agreement[4]

This employment agreement (the "Agreement") is made and entered into as of January 2, 2005, by and between Tree Services, Inc., a Colorado corporation (the "Company"), and Melissa Green, (the "Employee").

RECITALS

A. Prior to the date of this Agreement, Employee held the positions of Chief Executive Officer and President and Chairperson of the Board of Directors of the Company.

B. The Company desires to continue to employ the Employee, for an increased salary, from the date set forth above (the "Effective Date") until expiration of the term of this Agreement, and Employee is willing to be employed by Company during that period, on the terms and subject to the conditions set forth in this Agreement.

In consideration of the mutual covenants and promises of the parties, the Company and Employee covenant and agree as follows:

1. Duties

(a) During the term of this Agreement, Employee will be employed by the Company to serve as Chief Executive Officer and President of the Company. The Employee will devote a sufficient amount of business time to the conduct of the business of the Company as may be reasonably required to effectively discharge Employee's duties under this Agreement and, subject to the supervision and direction of the Company's Board of Directors (the "Board"), will perform those duties and have such authority and powers as are customarily associated with the offices of a Chief Executive Officer and President of a company engaged in a business that is similar to the business of the Company, including (without limitation): (a) the authority to direct and manage the day-to-day operations and affairs of the Company, (b) the authority to hire and discharge employees of the Company, and (c) all other authority and powers exercised by the Employee prior to the Effective Date as Chief Executive Officer of the Company; provided, however, that Employee will not be required to perform services for any affiliate of the Company and will not be required to accept any other offices with the Company without Employee's consent, which may be withheld at Employee's sole discretion. Unless the parties agree otherwise in writing, during the term of this Agreement, Employee will not be required to perform services under this

---

[4] This contract was adapted from *Executive Employment Agreement—Master Form with Commentary*, 16 Business Transactions Solutions §76:138 (last updated Feb. 2014).

Agreement other than at Company's principal place of business in Commerce City, Colorado or at such other location as Employee may choose from time to time to work from; provided, however, that Company may, from time to time, require Employee to travel temporarily to other locations on the Company's business. Notwithstanding the foregoing, nothing in this Agreement is to be construed as prohibiting Employee from continuing to serve as a director, officer or member of various professional, charitable and civic organizations in the same manner as immediately prior to the execution of this Agreement.

(b) Employee will be re-appointed to continue to serve as a member of the Board of Directors of Company (the "Board") as the Chairperson of the Board. At each annual meeting of the Company's shareholders during the term of employment, the Company will nominate Employee to serve as the Chairperson of the Board. Employee's service as the Chairperson of the Board will be subject to any required shareholder approval. Upon Termination for Cause of Employee's employment, Employee will be deemed to have resigned from the Board voluntarily, without any further required action by the Employee and Employee will, at the Board's request, execute any documents necessary to reflect her resignation.

2. Term of Employment

2.1. Definitions

For purposes of this Agreement the following terms have the following meanings:

(a) "Change in Control" means (a) one or more persons acquire beneficial ownership of the stock of the Company that, together with the stock held by such person or persons, constitutes more than 50% of the total voting power of the stock of the Company; provided, that, a Change in Control shall not occur if any person or persons owns more than 50% of the total voting power of the stock of the Company and acquires additional stock; (b) a majority of the members of the Board are replaced during any twelve-month period by directors whose appointment or election is not endorsed by a majority of the Board before the date of appointment or election; or (c) one person or persons acquires assets from the Company that have a total fair market value equal to or more than 40% of the total fair market value of all of the assets of the Company immediately before such acquisition.

(b) "Termination for Cause" means termination by Company of Employee's employment: (i) by reason of Employee's willful dishonesty towards, fraud upon, or deliberate injury to, the Company, (ii) by reason of Employee's on-going material breach of this Agreement, or (iii) by reason of Employee's gross negligence or intentional misconduct with respect to the performance of Employee's duties under this Agreement; provided, however, that no such termination will be deemed to be a Termination for Cause unless the Company has provided Employee with written notice of what it reasonably believes are the grounds for any Termination for Cause and Employee fails to take appropriate remedial actions during the 120-day period following receipt of such written notice.

(c) "Termination Other than For Cause" means termination by the Company of Employee's employment by the Company for reasons other than those, which constitute Termination for Cause.

(d) "Voluntary Termination" means termination by the Employee of the Employee's employment with the Company, excluding termination by reason of Employee's death or disability as described in Sections 2.5 and 2.6.

2.2. Basic Term

The term of employment of Employee by the Company will commence on the Effective Date and will extend indefinitely until terminated by Employee or Company pursuant to this Agreement, (the "Termination Date").

2.3. Termination for Cause

Termination for Cause may be effected by Company at any time during the term of this Agreement and may only be effected by written notification to Employee; provided, however, that no Termination for Cause will be effective unless Employee has been provided with the prior written notice and opportunity for remedial action described in Section 2.1. Upon Termination for Cause, Employee is to be immediately paid all accrued salary, incentive compensation to the extent earned, vested deferred compensation (other than pension plan or profit sharing plan benefits, which will be paid in accordance with the applicable plan), accrued vacation pay, and accrued sick pay, all to the date of termination, but Employee will not be paid any severance compensation.

2.4. Termination Other Than for Cause

Notwithstanding anything else in this Agreement, Company may effect a Termination Other Than for Cause at any time upon giving ninety (90) days prior written notice to Employee of such Termination Other Than for Cause. Upon any Termination Other Than for Cause, Employee will immediately be paid all accrued salary, all incentive compensation to the extent earned, severance compensation as provided in Section 4, vested deferred compensation (other than pension plan or profit sharing plan benefits, which will be paid in accordance with the applicable plan), accrued vacation pay, and accrued sick pay, all to the date of termination.

2.5. Termination Due to Disability

In the event that, during the term of this Agreement, Employee should, in the reasonable judgment of the Board, fail to perform Employee's duties under this Agreement because of illness or physical or mental incapacity ("Disability"), and such Disability continues for a period of more than twelve (12) consecutive months, Company will have the right to terminate Employee's employment under this Agreement by written notification to Employee and payment to Employee of all accrued salary and incentive compensation to the extent earned, severance compensation as provided in Section 4, vested deferred compensation (other than pension plan or profit sharing plan benefits, which will be paid in accordance with the applicable plan), all accrued vacation pay, and accrued sick pay, all to the date of termination. Any determination by the Board with respect to Employee's Disability must be based on a determination of competent medical authority or authorities, a copy of which determination must be delivered to the Employee at the time it is delivered to the Board. In the event the Employee disagrees with the determination described in the previous sentence, Employee will have the right to submit to the Board a determination by a competent medical authority or authorities of Employee's own choosing to the effect that the aforesaid determination is incorrect and that Employee is capable of performing Employee's duties under this Agreement. If, upon receipt of such determination, the Board wishes to continue to seek to terminate this Agreement under the provisions of this section, the parties will submit the issue of Employee's Disability to arbitration in accordance with the provisions of this Agreement.

2.6. Death

In the event of Employee's death during the term of this Agreement, Employee's employment is to be deemed to have terminated as of the last day of the month during which Employee's death occurred, and Company will pay to Employee's estate accrued salary, severance compensation as provided in Section 4, incentive compensation to the extent earned, vested deferred compensation (other than pension plan or profit sharing plan benefits, which will be paid in accordance with the applicable plan), accrued vacation pay, and accrued sick pay, all to the date of termination.

2.7. Voluntary Termination

In the event of a Voluntary Termination, Company will immediately pay to Employee all accrued salary, all incentive compensation to the extent earned, vested deferred compensation (other than pension plan or profit sharing plan benefits, which will be paid in accordance with the applicable plan), accrued vacation pay, and accrued sick pay, all to the date of termination, but Employee will not be paid any severance compensation.

3. Salary, Benefits, and Other Compensation

3.1. Base Salary

As payment for the services to be rendered by Employee as provided in Section 1 and subject to the terms and conditions of Section 2, Company agrees to pay to Employee a "Base Salary," payable monthly. The Base Salary payable to Employee under this Section will initially be $185,000. Employee will be entitled to regular salary reviews and raises during the term of this Agreement in the same general manner as other officers of the Company; provided, however, that Employee is entitled to receive a minimum annual increase in Employee's Base Salary of seven percent 5% per annum computed on the prior year's Base Salary. Furthermore, the Company and Employee acknowledge that, subject to the actual financial performance of the Company during the term of this Agreement, during the term of this Agreement it is the mutual intent of the parties that the Base Salary increase to a level that is commensurate with the level of compensation received by Employee for services rendered in an executive capacity for other entities prior to the commencement of Employee's employment with the Company.

3.2. Incentive Bonus Plans

During the term of her employment under this Agreement, the Employee will be eligible to participate in all bonus and incentive plans established by the Board.

3.3. Benefit Plans

During the term of Employee's employment under this Agreement, the Employee is to be eligible to participate in all employee benefit plans to the extent maintained by the Company, including (without limitation) any life, disability, health, accident and other insurance programs, paid vacations, and similar plans or programs, subject in each case to the generally applicable terms and conditions of the plan or program in question and to the determinations of any committee administering such plan or program. On termination of the Employee for any reason, the Employee will retain all of Employee's rights to benefits that have vested under such plan and Employee's rights of participation will continue for a period of two (2) years following Employee's termination.

3.4. Withholding of Taxes

The Employee understands that the services to be rendered by Employee under this Agreement will cause the Employee to recognize taxable income, which is considered under the Internal Revenue Code of 1986, as amended, and applicable regulations thereunder as compensation income subject to the withholding of income tax (and Social Security or other employment taxes). The Employee hereby consents to the withholding of such taxes as are required by the Company.

3.5. Vacation

During the term of this Agreement, Employee will be entitled to six (6) weeks paid vacation time per year.

3.6. Expenses

During the term of this Agreement, Company will reimburse Employee for Employee's reasonable out-of-pocket expenses incurred in connection with Company's business, including travel expenses, food, and lodging while away from home, subject to such policies as Company may from time to time reasonably establish for its employees. In addition, Company shall pay Employee a stipend in the amount of $1,500 for any Company related travel that exceeds three (3) calendar days.

3.7. Life Insurance

During the term of Employee's employment, the Company will pay for a $100,000 life insurance policy, in the form designated by Employee and approved by the Company's Board of Directors, covering the life of Employee and with proceeds payable to such beneficiaries as Employee designates. The foregoing is to be in addition to, and not in place of, any rights to which Employee's estate may be entitled under this Agreement on Employee's death. Upon any termination of Employee's employment, the aforementioned insurance policy will be assigned to the Employee and Employee will assume responsibility for all premium payments with respect the insurance policy; provided, however, that in the event that Employee's termination is as a result of a Termination Other Than for Cause, then the Company will continue to pay for premiums for the insurance policy for a period of two (2) years from the date of Employee's termination.

4. Severance Compensation

4.1. Termination Other Than for Cause; Payment in Lieu of Notice

In the event Employee's employment is involuntarily terminated in a Termination Other Than for Cause while holding Executive Officer status or within one hundred eighty (180) days of having held Executive Officer status, Employee will be entitled to the following severance pay:

    (a)   a lump sum severance payment in an amount equivalent, before taxes and other deductions, to 3.0 times the sum of her current annual base salary and annual target cash bonus, both as in effect immediately prior to separation from employment.

4.2. Termination for Disability or Death

In the event Employee's employment is terminated because of Employee's disability pursuant to Section 2.5 or death pursuant to Section 2.6, Employee or Employee's estate will be entitled to the following severance pay:

    (a)   a lump sum severance payment in an amount equivalent, before taxes and other deductions, to 3.0 times the sum of her current annual base salary and annual target cash bonus, both as in effect immediately prior to separation from employment.

4.3. Other Termination

In the event of a Voluntary Termination or Termination for Cause, Employee or Employee's estate will not be entitled to any severance pay.

5. Confidentiality and Noncompetition

5.1. Confidentiality

Because of Employee's employment by Company, Employee will have access to trade secrets and confidential information about Company, its products, its customers, and its methods of doing business (the "Confidential Information"). During and after the termination of Employee's employment by the Company, Employee may not directly or indirectly disclose or use any such Confidential Information; provided, that Employee will not incur any liability for disclosure of information which: (a) is required in the course of Employee's employment by the Company, (b) was permitted in writing by the

Board, or (c) is within the public domain or comes within the public domain without any breach of this Agreement.

5.2. Noncompetition

In consideration of Employee's access to the Confidential Information, Employee agrees that for a period of six (6) months after termination of Employee's employment, Employee will not, directly or indirectly, use such Confidential Information to compete with the business of the Company, as the business of the Company may then be constituted, within any state, region or locality in which the Company is then doing business or marketing its products. Employee understands and agrees that direct competition means development, production, promotion, or sale of products or services competitive with those of Company. Indirect competition means employment by any competitor or third party providing products or services competing with Company's products or services, for whom Employee will perform the same or similar function as he performs for Company. In addition, for a period of six (6) months after termination of Employee's employment, Employee will not induce or attempt to induce any employee of the Company to discontinue his or her employment with the Company for the purpose of becoming employed by any competitor of Company, nor will Employee initiate discussions, negotiations or contacts with persons known by Employee to be a customer or supplier of the Company at the time of Employee's termination of employment for the purpose of competing with the Company.

Notwithstanding anything to the contrary contained in the Agreement, the provisions of this Section 5.2 will not be applicable in the event of any Termination Other Than for Cause with respect to Employee.

6. Assignment of Inventions

All processes, inventions, patents, copyrights, trademarks, and other intangible rights (collectively the "Inventions") that may be conceived or developed by Employee, either alone or with others, during the term of Employee's employment, whether or not conceived or developed during Employee's working hours, and with respect to which the equipment, supplies, facilities, or trade secret information of Company was used, or that relate at the time of conception or reduction to practice of the Invention to the business of the Company or to Company's actual or demonstrably anticipated research and development, or that result from any work performed by Employee for Company, will be the sole property of Company, and Employee hereby assigns to the Company all of Employee's right, title and interest in and to such Inventions. Employee must disclose to Company all inventions conceived during the term of employment, whether or not the invention constitutes property of Company under the terms of the preceding sentence, but such disclosure will be received by Company in confidence. Employee must execute all documents, including patent applications and assignments, required by Company to establish Company's rights under this Section.

7. Change in Control

Upon a Change in Control, Company shall:

(a) pay Employee as of the date of the Change in Control a lump-sum cash bonus equal to four times her total annual compensation, comprised of salary and bonuses prior to any elective deferrals or any other deductions, paid in the calendar year immediately preceding the Change in Control, such payment to be in lieu of the cash payments payable under Section 4.1.

(b) make available to Employee the retiree benefits specified in Section 3.3.

8. Miscellaneous

8.1. Waiver

The waiver of any breach of any provision of this Agreement will not operate or be construed as a waiver of any subsequent breach of the same or other provision of this Agreement.

8.2. Entire Agreement; Modification

Except as otherwise provided in the Agreement, this Agreement represents the entire understanding among the parties with respect to the subject matter of this Agreement, and this Agreement supersedes any and all prior understandings, agreements, plans, and negotiations, whether written or oral, with respect to the subject matter hereof, including without limitation, any understandings, agreements, or obligations respecting any past or future compensation, bonuses, reimbursements, or other payments to Employee from Company. All modifications to the Agreement must be in writing and signed by the party against whom enforcement of such modification is sought.

8.3. Notice

All notices and other communications under this Agreement must be in writing and must be given by personal delivery, electronic delivery, or first class mail, certified or registered with return receipt requested, and will be deemed to have been duly given upon receipt if personally delivered, one hour after being sent if electronically delivered, or three days after mailing, if mailed, to the respective persons named below:

If to Company: Tree Services, Inc.
6789 120th Street
Commerce City, CO 80022
Attn: Thomas Shrub

If to Employee: Melissa Green
11111 18th Street
Denver, CO 80202

Any party may change such party's address for notices by notice duly given pursuant to this Section.

8.4. Headings

The Section headings of this Agreement are intended for reference and may not by themselves determine the construction or interpretation of this Agreement.

8.5. Governing Law

This Agreement is to be governed by and construed in accordance with the laws of the State of Colorado applicable to contracts entered into and wholly to be performed within the State of Colorado by Colorado residents. Any controversy or claim arising out of or relating to this Agreement, or breach of this Agreement (except any controversy or claim with respect to Section 5 or 6), is to be settled by arbitration in Denver, Colorado in accordance with the Commercial Arbitration Rules of the American Arbitration Association, and judgment on the award rendered by the arbitrators may be entered in any court having jurisdiction. There must be three arbitrators, one to be chosen directly by each party at will, and the third arbitrator to be selected by the two arbitrators so chosen. Each party will pay the fees of the arbitrator he or she selects and his or her own attorneys, and the expenses of his or her witnesses and all other expenses connected with presenting his or her case. Other costs of the arbitration, including the cost of any record or transcripts of the arbitration, administrative fees, the fee of the third arbitrator, and all other fees and costs, will be borne equally by the parties. Notwithstanding anything in this Agreement to the contrary, if any controversy or claim arises between the parties under Section 5 or 6 of this Agreement, the Company will not be required to arbitrate that controversy or claim but the Company will have the right to institute judicial proceedings in any court of competent jurisdiction with respect to such controversy or claim. If such judicial proceedings are instituted, the parties agree that such proceedings will not be stayed or delayed pending the outcome of any arbitration proceeding under this Agreement.

8.6. Survival of Company's Obligations

This Agreement will be binding on, and inure to the benefit of, the executors, administrators, heirs, successors, and assigns of the parties; provided, however, that except as expressly provided in this Agreement, this Agreement may not be assigned either by Company or by Employee.

8.7. Counterparts

This Agreement may be executed in one or more counterparts, all of which taken together will constitute one and the same Agreement.

8.8. Withholdings

All sums payable to Employee under this Agreement will be reduced by all federal, state, local, and other withholdings and similar taxes and payments required by applicable law.

8.9. Enforcement

If any portion of this Agreement is determined to be invalid or unenforceable, that portion of this Agreement will be adjusted, rather than voided, to achieve the intent of the parties under this Agreement.

8.10. Indemnification

The Company agrees that it will indemnify and hold the Employee harmless to the fullest extent permitted by applicable law from and against any loss, cost, expense or liability resulting from or by reason of the fact of the Employee's employment hereunder, whether as an officer, employee, agent, fiduciary, director or other official of the Company, except to the extent of any expenses, costs, judgments, fines or settlement amounts which result from conduct which is determined by a court of competent jurisdiction to be knowingly and grossly fraudulent or deliberately dishonest or to constitute some other type of grossly willful misconduct.

IN WITNESS WHEREOF, the parties hereto have executed this Agreement as of the day and year first above written.

Tree Services, Inc.

By: _____ /s/ Thomas Shrub _____
           Thomas Shrub, CFO

EMPLOYEE

By: _____ /s/ Melissa Green _____
           Melissa Green, CEO & President

TSI's Form Services Agreement

TSI's FORM
SERVICES AGREEMENT[5]

THIS AGREEMENT is made and entered into this _____ day of _____, 20_____ by and between [name of owner] ("Owner"), and Tree Services, Inc., a Colorado corporation having an office at 6789 120th Street, Commerce City, CO 80022 ("TSI");

WITNESSETH:

WHEREAS, Owner owns, operates, and/or manages the premises located at _____, _____, Colorado (the Property); and

WHEREAS, TSI is in the business of providing landscaping services to residential and commercial real estate owners, operators, and managers; and

WHEREAS, the parties have agreed that TSI shall provide such landscaping services, all for the consideration, and upon the terms, provisions, and conditions set forth herein;

NOW, THEREFORE, in consideration of the premises, the covenants, and the agreements herein contained, and other good and valuable consideration, the receipt of which is acknowledged, the parties agree as follows:

Landscaping.

Section 1. Landscaping. Owner hereby employs and hires Company to provide landscaping services at the Property and Company agrees to provide such services pursuant to the terms and conditions hereinafter set forth:

    (a) TSI will perform weekly landscaping maintenance commencing April 1st and ending October 31st during each year of the Agreement.

    (b) The weekly maintenance program will include: (i) weekly cutting of all grass areas; (ii) edging of all walkways and shrub borders; (iii) maintenance of all trees and shrubs on the property; (iv) weed control of shrub and tree beds; (v) fertilization and disease control of shrubs and trees, when necessary; (vi) pruning of shrubs and trees, when necessary; and (vii) cleaning of walkways, following servicing of the landscaped areas.

---

[5] This contract was adapted from *Form of Landscape Maintenance Agreement*, 23 West's Legal Forms, Real Estate Transactions, Commercial §50:1.

(c) TSI shall provide for the following chemical applications and services: (i) in April, crabgrass prevention, fertilizer, grub and other disease control applications, and deep root watering; (ii) in May, fertilizer application and deep root watering; (iii) in June, broad leaf weed control application and deep root watering; (iv) in July and August, insecticide application and deep root watering; (v) in September, fertilizer, insecticide, grub and disease control, broad leaf weed control applications, and deep root watering; and (vi) in October, fertilization application, and tree and shrub pruning and shaping.

(d) The weekly maintenance program shall not include the following items: (i) seeding or sodding any grass areas which need replacement; (ii) replacement of dead shrubs and trees; (iii) replacement of mulch in beds; (iv) cleanup of landscaped areas before April 1st or after October 31st during each year of the Agreement.

(e) In the event that any service(s) or supplies in addition to that described in (a) to (d) above are requested by Owner, TSI will provide same and shall receive, as payment for such additional service(s) or supplies, compensation comparable to charges by other maintenance companies offering the same range of services and qualified personnel in the area. Owner shall render, along with such payments, sales tax at the rate of 7.62%.

Compensation.

Section 2. Compensation. TSI shall receive, as full payment for all landscaping services performed under this Agreement, an annual amount as follows: for the first year, the amount shall be $[dollar amount of payment]; thereafter, the amount shall be adjusted on an annual basis, based upon increases to the "Consumer Price Index for Urban Consumers" published by the Bureau of Labor Statistics of the United States Department of Labor, for the City of Denver, all Items ([number of price]-100), or a successor or substitute index appropriately adjusted (the "Price Index"), over the price index for the Base Year. This Base Year index shall mean the average of the monthly All Items Price Index for each of the 12 months of the Base Year (the Base Year being the full calendar year in which the term of the Agreement commences). The increase shall take effect as of the anniversary date of the Agreement. The annual adjustment shall be based upon the percentage difference between the Price Index for the calendar month immediately preceding the anniversary date of the Agreement and the price index for the Base Year. The adjusted annual amount shall be payable in equal monthly installments until it is readjusted pursuant to the terms of the Agreement. In the event that this Agreement is renewed, as provided in Section 8 of this Agreement, the annual amount shall be adjusted during such renewal year in accordance with the foregoing terms. The Base Year index (the Base Year being the full calendar year in which the term of this Agreement commenced) shall be used for purposes of determining the annual amount due during any renewal year.

Notwithstanding the foregoing, it is agreed that the adjusted annual amount shall in no event be less than $250 per annum.

Sales Tax.

Section 3. Sales Tax. This Agreement is subject to sales tax, which is based upon 7.62% of the annual compensation which is due and owing during each year of the Agreement as calculated pursuant to Section 2 plus any additional compensation due pursuant to Section 1(e) above. The annual amount of sales tax shall be payable by Owner in equal monthly installments, along with the monthly installments of the annual compensation payable pursuant to Section 2 and Section 1(e) hereof.

Discounts.

(optional section for most favored customers)

Option 1:

Section 4: Discounts. Not applicable.

Option 2:

Section 4: Discounts. In the event that Owner contracts for services that exceed $1,000 per month for a minimum term of six months, starting in the seventh month Owner shall be eligible for up to a 3% discount off the total compensation due TSI pursuant to Section 2 above. In order to receive the 3% discount off total compensation due TSI, Owner must pay its monthly invoice within five (5) business days by electronic funds transfer or some other form of automated payment. In the event that Owner pays the invoice later than five (5) business days, Owner is not eligible for the 5% monthly discount.

Option 3:

Section 4: Discounts. In the event that Owner contracts for services that exceed $1,500 per month for a minimum term of six months, starting in the seventh month Owner shall be eligible for up to a 5% discount off the total compensation due TSI pursuant to Section 2 above. In order to receive the 5% discount off total compensation due TSI, Owner must pay its monthly invoice within five (5) business days by electronic funds transfer or some other form of automated payment.

In the event that Owner pays the invoice later than five (5) business days, Owner is not eligible for the 5% monthly discount.

Option 4 (only for TSI's top 30 customers):

Section 4. [TSI may include terms that provide these customers with larger discounts, better payment terms, lower default interest rates, and a customer referral bonus as it deems necessary].

Insurance.

Section 5. Insurance. TSI shall, at all times, keep in full force and effect: (i) comprehensive general liability insurance, on an occurrence basis, of not less than $1 million for personal injury and $50,000 for property damage; and (ii) Workers' Compensation and Disability insurance covering its employees.

Independent Contractor.

Section 6. Independent Contractor. TSI shall, for all purposes, be deemed an independent contractor, rather than an agent of Owner and TSI agrees that it shall not hold itself out to third parties other than as an independent contractor.

Indemnification.

Section 7. Indemnification. TSI shall not be liable to Owner for any loss or damage, unless caused by Maintainer's own gross negligence or misconduct. Owner agrees to indemnify and hold harmless TSI for any liability, damages, costs, and expenses (including reasonable attorney's fees, costs, and disbursements) sustained or incurred for injury to any person or damage to any property in, about, and in connection with the Property, from any cause whatsoever, unless such injury shall be caused by Maintainer's own gross negligence or misconduct.

Term, Termination of Agreement.

Section 8. Term, Termination of Agreement. This Agreement shall be in effect for a term of one (1) year from the date set forth in the introductory paragraph.

This Agreement will be renewed automatically from year to year following its expiration, unless canceled by either party upon the giving of at least ninety (90) days' prior written notice. The annual amount due during any renewal year shall be determined in accordance with Section 5 of this Agreement.

This Agreement is subject, however, to the right of TSI to terminate this Agreement for any reason, or for no reason, at the end of any calendar month, upon the giving of at least thirty (30) days' prior written notice.

Notices.

Section 9. Notices. All communications, notices, and demands of any kind which either party may be required or desire to give or serve upon the other party shall be made in writing, and shall be delivered electronically or by personal service to an officer of the other party or sent by certified mail, return receipt requested, to the following addressee:

If to Owner: [Address of Owner]
                 [City, State, Zip]
                 [Attention: _____]

If to TSI: 6789 120th Street
                 Commerce City, CO 80022
                 Attn: Thomas Shrub

Any such notices sent by mail shall be presumed to have been received by the addressee four (4) business days after posting in the United States mail. Either party may change its address by giving the other party written notice of its new address as provided herein.

Late or Default in Payments.

Section 10. Late or Default in Payments. In the event that Owner does not pay its monthly invoice within fifteen (15) days, all amounts overdue shall accrue interest at the rate of twelve percent (12%). In addition, in the event that Owner defaults in making any payments required hereunder, and TSI engages an attorney, collection agent, or other agency for collection of such payments, then the balance due herein shall be increased by an additional fifteen percent (15%) for reasonable attorney's fees.

Assignment.

Section 11. Assignment. This Agreement may be assigned by TSI at any time, upon the giving of ten (10) days' notice to Owner.

Entire Agreement, Amendments.

Section 12. Entire Agreement, Amendments. This Agreement and the items incorporated herein contain all of the agreement of the parties hereto with respect to the matters contained herein, and no prior agreement or understanding pertaining to any such matter shall be effective. No provisions of this Agreement may be amended or modified in any manner whatsoever.

Captions.

Section 13. Captions. Captions to articles, sections, and paragraphs of this Agreement are not a part of this Agreement and shall not be deemed to affect the meaning or construction of any of its provisions.

Severability.

Section 14. Severability. If any term or provision of this Agreement, or the application thereof, to any person or circumstance shall, to any extent, be invalid or unenforceable, the remaining terms and provisions of this Agreement, or the application of such terms or provisions to the person or circumstances, other than those as to which it is held invalid or unenforceable, shall not be affected thereby, and each term and provision of this Agreement shall be valid and shall be enforced to the fullest extent permitted by law.

Governing Law.

Section 15. Governing Law. This Agreement shall be construed in accordance with the laws, including the conflict of law rules, of the State of California.

Force Majeure

Section 16. Force Majeure. TSI shall not be responsible or liable to Owner, nor be deemed to have defaulted under or breached this Agreement, for any failure or delay in fulfilling or performing any term of this Agreement when and to the extent such failure or delay is caused by or results from acts beyond TSI's reasonable control, including without limitation (i) acts of God; (ii) flood, fire, or earthquake; (iii) war, invasion, hostilities, terrorist threats or acts, riot or other civil unrest; (iv) government order or law; (v) national or regional emergency; or (vi) other similar events or circumstances. TSI shall promptly give notice of the force majeure event to Owner.

IN WITNESS WHEREOF, the parties have caused this Agreement to be executed by their duly authorized representatives.

[Name of owner]

By:_____   Date:_____
  [Name of authorized representative]
  [Title of authorized representative]

Tree Services, Inc.

By:_____   Date:_____
        Melissa Green
        CEO & President

APPENDIX C

CHAPTER 20—SUPPLEMENTAL CLASS EXERCISE HANDOUT

■ ■ ■

Mr. Fred Bachrach
President, Big Homes For Big Bucks, Inc.
816 Swansong Ave.
Leadville, Colorado

Re: Unpaid Invoices amounting to over $35,000 for which you are inappropriately delinquent

Fred:

I represent the entity that provided the piping for your most recent residential project, Consolidated Pipe and Sweat. Pursuant to your agreement with CPS you owe CPS a lot of money. I believe you are well aware of this fact. CPS is a long standing client and excellent customer of our firm. Please know we will take all necessary actions for our client.

On or about the middle of the year before last, CPS began work on your project. CPS provided all of the materials and labor for the entire build, from beginning to end. Although you routinely made unreasonable demands that forced my client to go above and beyond the call of duty to meet your requirements, CPS continued to service your project. However, any gratitude from you seems to be lacking. The project ended about 6 months ago, and quite a few invoices remain unpaid. Over the time CPS worked on the project you racked up bills in materials, labor, and change orders that amounted to well over $35,000. That's a lot of money, Fred. I understand that you don't think the change orders are appropriate. However, pursuant to the agreement that you yourself signed, they are completely acceptable with the contract. Dave informed me of the number of incidents he had with Carl relative to the changes in scope, but Carl is not the signing authority on the agreement. And the agreement fully contemplated surcharges for change orders. You know this. Additionally, Dave informed me that he did receive the check from you for $12,037 that you said you sent two weeks ago. What are you playing at with that?

Given the forgoing, you are clearly in breach of your agreement with CSP. Also given the forgoing, you aren't very good at math, but I bet you're good enough to figure out how much the lawsuit will cost you when Dave rips open the walls of that newly occupied home to tear out his pipes.

Obviously, no one wants that to happen. We'd rather you just cure your breach. We need the balance between what you've paid to date and what you owe. This needs to be paid within 10 days in the customary fashion. If it is not paid we will be forced to pursue other options available to us that I can assure you, will NOT be pleasant.

Thank you for your prompt attention to this matter.

Sincerely,

/S/

Ruprecht Hagen, esq.
Partner
Hagen, Horowitz, and Hanover, LLP

INDEX

References are to Pages
